PLAYFUL
MIND

PLAYFUL MIND

BRINGING CREATIVITY TO LIFE

JAMES DOWNTON, JR.

Humanics Trade Group
Atlanta, GA USA

HUMANICS

Playful Mind
A Humanics Trade Group Publication

Humanics trade Group Publications are an imprint of and published by Humanics Publishing Group, a division of Brumby Holdings, Inc. Its trademark, consisting of the words "Humanics Trade Group" and a portrayal of a Pegasus, is registered in the U.S. Patent Office and in other countries.

Brumby Holdings, Inc.
1197 Peachtree St.
Suite 533B Plaza
Atlanta, GA 30361
USA

Printed in the United States of America and the United Kingdom

Library of Congress Control Number: 2002104838
ISBN (Paperback): 0-89334-358-7
ISBN (Hardcover): 0-89334-359-5

DEDICATION

For my students,
who cultivated
more creative lives
by practicing
the principles of this work.

What you accomplished
inspires me.

The way you changed confirms the idea
that all humans are creative
and
they cannot help it.

PLAYFUL MIND:
*"It's hard to dance in tight jeans
—also true of tight mind."*

CONTENTS

our chances of realizing our dreams.

Chapter 5: You Are Gifted 29

Many of us are keenly aware of other peoples' creative gifts, but not our own. Acknowledging our gifts and adding new ones, we become more resourceful so our creativity is cultivated with greater freedom and enthusiasm.

Chapter 6: Take Risks 35

As children, coloring inside the lines was applauded. We were, and still are, pressured to conform. The "guardians" of convention may hold us back. Sometimes we restrict ourselves. By discovering what limits our creativity, we take risks and try out new ideas.

Chapter 7: Small Changes Can Produce Big Results 45

Creative plans can become so grandiose, our efforts collapse under their weight. In contrast, by adding and subtracting one little thing, we can produce significant results. One thing we add is our "life purposes," which gives our creativity new direction and meaning.

Chapter 8: Managing Your Fears 49

Creativity can be frightening because of its risks. Many fears arise from our desire to impress others so we can feel good about ourselves. When we express ourselves rather than trying to impress others, our fears diminish so we feel freer to take risks and create.

Chapter 9: You Can Create Inspiration 55

Creativity can stall because we lose inspiration. We wait for a Muse to bring us the gift of creative fire. The waiting can stop. In an instant, we can create our own inspiration. Using "inspiration points," new ideas comes quickly, which makes us and the Muse happy.

Chapter 10: Use Imagination To Free Your Mind 59

Nothing frees the mind faster than imagination. "Let's pretend," "What if?", and "Future stretch" are ways of awakening imagination. When our imaginations are active, so is playful mind. Together, they dream up novel ideas in abundance.

The mind becomes dull when it grows comfortable with its normal way of thinking. When a new issue arises, it falls into its old perspective. By using the techniques of "Mind Switching" and "Roleling Around," we learn to shift perspectives and create innovations in our thinking.

Assumptions are the invisible bars of our thinking prisons. Being invisible, we no longer question them. By becoming aware of our assumptions and how they restrict our thinking, we break out of our mental confinement to develop fresh ideas.

Creativity can become a competitive sport. We may try to make creativity points or take credit for ideas and results. There is a cooperative alternative to this approach which emphasizes co-creation. We learn to co-create with others without competing for recognition.

To insure effectiveness, Walt Disney invented three rooms. The dream room inspired imagination, the planning room stressed careful design, and the critic's room was where plans were evaluated and refined. By visiting those rooms, we find it easier to create good results.

Creativity is sometimes stopped by negative thoughts we think are true. Once this is understood, we develop the capacity to stop those thoughts from stopping us. By cultivating this ability, we are able to maintain our creative momentum in the face of many obstacles.

Many of us cannot take criticism. We become defensive, fight back, and miss the feedback. The information that would allow us to learn and change is missed. By enhancing our ability to be coached, we quickly increase our creative capacity and effectiveness.

How do we know when our minds have achieved playfulness? By answering the question, "What's in the box?" With a more playful mind, we are able to cultivate more abundance in our lives, which includes more adventure, fun, and fulfillment.

Appreciation

I want to thank those who responded so openly to this work in my creativity class and in community workshops. I appreciate their willingness to change and move into creative action. Many began thinking they were not creative and now know they cannot help it. What they accomplished would impress anyone. Through their efforts, their creativity has blossomed.

Many people have influenced this work. Don Lambert's creativity had a major impact on my thinking when we worked together. His playful mind is alive in some of the chapters.

Barbara Kelly made an important contribution to the editing of the manuscript. Her coaching to use fewer words to express my ideas was invaluable. My wife Mary is one of my best coaches. Her willingness to give honest and constructive feedback always improves my work.

My art teachers helped me develop my creative and technical skills, which increased the fun I have while painting and sculpting. Practicing the principles of this book in my art, where I was often tempted to give up, helped me see the great utility of those principles. Other influences came from classes I took from Landmark Education, an organization devoted to transforming the lives of people. To learn more, visit its website at [www.landmarkeducation.com].

Creativity is often associated with the arts, but that is a small part of its domain. Creativity is about cultivating playful mind and the ability to realize dreams in any part of life. Social change is creativity work. I want to appreciate the many people whose values lead them to creativity as a way to help others. They create organizations and projects that improve the lives of others so life can flourish. One such organization is Girls, Inc. The people in that organization offer opportunities for young and teenaged girls to learn skills that create self-confidence, better opportunities, and much brighter futures. Half of my royalties from *Playful Mind* will go to Girls, Inc. To learn more about its good work, see page 155 at the back of this book and explore its website [www.girlsinc.org].

WE LIVE IN MIND BOXES

When people tell me that they are not creative, I ask "How did you learn to think that way?" Some recall a teacher or parent who conveyed this message to them, which they embraced as the truth. Others developed the belief by comparing themselves to sisters or brothers who were recognized as creative, or to people whose creative talents they used as a standard against which they evaluated their own. Other peoples' opinions, but most importantly their own, led them to turn off the creativity they expressed so freely as children. Believing they were not endowed with creativity, their lives lost some of its zest and adventure. This loss can occur at any age.

Wendy's creative spirit had disappeared by the time she was twenty-five. She had convinced herself that she was not creative, so she held back anytime we were doing creative work together. She sat at a safe distance judging everyone harshly because she was severely judging herself. I knew I had to do something to change her thinking so I drew her aside one day and asked, "When are you going to take off the judge's robe and get involved?"

She was surprised by my directness, but once I explained what I was observing, she admitted that I was right. Then I asked "Who is getting your most severe judgment?" "Me," she said. "So, what will it take for you to stop judging yourself?" She thought about my question for a moment. "A willingness to try," she said. From that day on, she suspended judgment and tried. Soon, she was creating amazing things. Her friends began to notice the change in her which reinforced the idea that she was creative. Before long, she was fully launched into a more creative life and she loved it.

What is "creativity"? Creativity is the capacity to think and live in novel ways. It is the ability to imagine, to courageously pursue goals, and to think with a playful mind. Playful mind is the bold and free spirit within us that loves flexibility, risk-taking, and the adventure of exploring. It creates surprises and shifts in our thinking, so we receive new and unusual ideas with little effort.

PLAYFUL MIND:
*"Imagine your life is a playground,
not a proving ground!"*

The creative process is simple. When the following principles are embraced, we keep creativity in motion.

Do,
Get feedback through "mistakes,"
Learn from the feedback,
Change what you are doing.

People sometimes ask me if creativity can be restored and expanded. My answer is always an emphatic "Yes!" Creativity can be revitalized because we are gifted with awareness, the ability to choose, and the capacity to change. This gives us the power to become more flexible and playful in our thinking. Once we understand what stops our creativity, we can become unstoppable. This ability to maintain creative momentum improves our chances of creating nourishing relationships, a career that is fascinating, and an enjoyable life. In its broadest sweep, creativity is about who we declare ourselves to be and how we choose to live. By claiming creativity as a core value, our lives become more intriguing, vital, and fun.

During more than twenty years of teaching creativity, I have seen many people change from thinking "I'm not creative" to becoming unstoppable in the creative realm. By working through the learning processes of this book, they recover playful mind, so they become more flexible and innovative in the way they think and live. Their effectiveness as planners increases. so they get better results. Many experience an abrupt increase in confidence and well-being. Their experiences are included as examples, but I have changed their names to conceal their identities.

The best way to experience this book is with a group of people or a partner, although significant results can be achieved working alone. To create a complete range of options, the exercises are designed for individuals, partners, or groups. If you work alone, you will need a partner on a few occasions.

Use the book in a way that works best for you, cover to cover or by focusing on chapters that seem most important. Take time between chapters to digest the work and to practice the principles. Keep on track, but move slowly enough so that deep learning occurs. Practice putting creativity into different parts of your life. The point is to make creativity a central part of who you are and how you live.

The Woo Way: A New Way Of Living And Being is another book in The Life Gardening Project. It works in harmony with *Playful Mind* to enhance the meaning and quality of life. To learn more, visit The Life Gardening Project on the web: [http://lifegardening.com].

For additional reading, I recommend any work by Sark. Her books, such as *Living Juicy, Inspiration Sandwich*, and *Succulent Wild Woman*, cultivate a more playful mind. Also, consider the fun you will have with Roger Von Oech's *Creative Whack Pack*, cards that add creativity to thinking. For a different experiential approach to creativity, explore Julia Cameron's *The Artist's Way*.

Rough time limits for the processes are noted. If you are working alone, set your own limits. If you are working with a partner, the time limits should be determined together. Groups can assign a facilitator for each chapter to guide the work. Use the designated time limits as a rough gauge, but be prepared to pace the work according to individual and group needs. Partner and group sharing will add time to each process.

Purchase a large journal for doing the experiential work, writing prose and poetry, and planning. With journal in hand, create a title that challenges you to expand your creativity. Buy colored pens, crayons, and a large pad of paper.

The words of playful mind, poems, bumper stickers, and similar inventions come from me. They are part of the fun I had while writing.

I invite you into this work with a promise that, if you do the processes, you will cultivate more creativity in your life. A haiku captures this possibility.

> *The water turned up.*
> *The creative life restored.*
> *A new garden grows.*

Chapter 1

YOU BECOME WHO YOU SAY YOU ARE

Playful mind is imprisoned by the stories we tell about ourselves. Embedded in those stories are beliefs we never question because we are convinced that they are "true." Those beliefs shape our identity and confine what we can perceive, think, and do. A seasoned teacher once said: "We speak our worlds into existence. Who we declare ourselves to be, we become. Only when those stories are challenged is a change of identity possible. Most of us fail to realize that we are just a good book of fiction that can be revised. Everything is brought into existence through language. Change the words, we change ourselves."

Jerry Hirshberg talks about creativity as "effective surprise" in *The Creative Priority*. He says that the mind is surprised at a deep level when the beliefs that support its sense of certainty are suspended. This may cause confusion, yet new opportunities also appear for making positive changes. By rejecting the truth of our beliefs, the barriers that restrict what we see, think, and do are torn down. When this demolition project is completed, we awaken new ideas and novel approaches come quickly to mind.

PLAYFUL MIND:
*"Instead of thinking of yourself as a melodrama,
consider yourself a comic book."*

Individual Process (20 minutes): Tear up a sheet of paper into ten parts. On each slip, identify a personal attribute that describes your deepest sense of identity. For example, someone might write "helpful" on one slip, "sincere" on another. Include less positive attributes if they are important. Maybe "difficult," "moody," "self-conscious," "eager to please" are possibilities.

Create a triangular pattern with your attributes, placing your most defining attribute at the top. The next two important qualities would go on the second line, with the trait on the left having the greater influence. Move your attributes around until you achieve a pattern that most clearly captures the way you see yourself, not how you want to be seen.

Focusing on your work, write a brief personal advertisement of yourself. It might read, "Kind, moody but interesting, woman who is also...."

If you are working with a partner or group, read your ads to each other. Discuss what you are noticing about your identity.

*Cultivate a change of identity so
more creativity can grow in your life.*

Individual Process (15 minutes): Look through your attributes to see if "creative" appears. If it does, where have you placed it? Do you see it as a core part of your identity or less influential? Reflect on the question: "How does saying I am creative affect how I feel as a person and what I undertake in my life?" If "creative" is not your top attribute, put it alongside your other leading trait. This simple change will create a shift of focus within your identity.

If you want, you can put "creative" alone at the top to discover what happens.

If "creative" was completely absent, think about why and whether you would like it to be present. Decide to add "creative" to what you say about yourself. Out of curiosity, put it at the top alongside your leading trait.

With "creative" at the top, examine the rest of your traits. Which ones would strengthen your creativity? Move them toward the top. For example, an ability like "persistent" would strengthen creativity, so it would be moved up. Rearrange your pattern by moving all attributes that would support your creativity toward the top.

On separate slips of paper, indicate any new attributes that would support a creative identity. "Courageous" comes to mind or "risk-taker." Add those new qualities to the pattern where their impact would be greatest.

Recess of the mind: Examine your new identity. Imagine what it would be like to live in that new story. What would be added to your life? What would disappear? What would you undertake that your former identity omitted as a possibility?

Individual Process (10 minutes): With your new identity, write another advertisement.

When you finish, compare this ad to your earlier one. What differences do you see? Which of these identities is more appealing to you? What makes it more appealing?

If you are working with a partner or group, read your new advertisements to each other.

PLAYFUL MIND:
"Since social life is primarily sales work, why not
become a creative product others will find
interesting, useful, and fun?"

Create A New Name

In *Wildmind*, Natalie Goldberg recommends that writers create a new name and identity for themselves to enrich their imaginations and to take greater risks in their writing. You are at a similar crossroads with playful mind. A new name to express your creative identity will free you to be more innovative and courageous in the way you think and live.

Individual Process (10 minutes): Invent a new name for your creative self. It might be "Stretch" or something fanciful like "Yog." Maybe you would like to make a slight change in your own name. I remember when "Joe" changed his name to "Joey" so he could think more playfully. He felt too serious and restricted as "Joe" and freer as "Joey."

Once you have established your new name, record it in your journal. Afterwards, imagine yourself living with your new name. How will you feel? What will you try that you had not considered before? What new creative risks will you take?

If you are working with a partner or group, share your new name and how it will help you to cultivate more creativity in your life. How will it increase your power to create?

Yasmin is naturally fun and creative. Yet, being human, she

has her fears. To counteract them, she developed a creative alter ego called "Citrus." She went further by dressing as Citrus in a bright orange wig, a flashy orange dress, and orange running shoes. As Citrus, Yasmin could be brave. As a challenge, she volunteered to lead a creativity workshop for sixty people at a leadership conference, which was something she had never done before. As the date of the conference approached, her fears took over. She began to think of many reasons for not doing it, until, one day she said to herself, "I know I can't do it, but Citrus can." On the day of the workshop, she appeared as Citrus wearing her bright orange wig, dress and running shoes. As Citrus, Yasmin enjoyed the challenge of stimulating people's creativity. Participants' evaluations indicated the workshop was very effective.

Chapter 2

LET YOUR MIND PLAY

*E*xpanding creativity is like being invited onto the starship Enterprise to go where no one has dared to go before. Can you feel the excitement of uncharted space? Smell the joy of exploration? Taste the challenge of change? Touch what is still unawakened? See infinite possibilities? Our journey begins with our master computer locked onto our ultimate destination, the unexplored territory of playful mind. To get there, we learn to practice the "Fun-da-mentals of Creative Thinking," where the "fun" always comes before the "mental."

The Fun-da-mentals

When the fun-da-mentals of creative thinking are practiced, you will produce a sudden expansion in your ability to create new and sometimes weird ideas.

■ Experience failures as feedback.

Many of us become mentally frozen by our fear of failure. When fear tightens our minds, we become too serious and overly cautious. In this rigid state, we miss the opportunity to let our minds play. To develop a more playful mind, think "feedback" anytime "failure" comes to mind. Failures are just feedback to help you learn.

■ Take risks.

When we have a risky idea and fail to act on it, we miss the opportunity to satisfy our curiosity. Instead of thinking that risk is dangerous, treat it as an opportunity to discover or develop something new. Imagine naming a mortuary "The Next to the Last Stop" or "Place Your Bet." These names would be risky, but they might also attract a lot of business. Notice that risk-taking is when the feeling of adventure begins for you.

■ Stop trying so hard to impress others.

Independence has a better chance of producing new ideas and results than conformity. Consider how our thinking and behavior are limited by what we think others will say about it. This over-sensitivity to people's opinions leads us to relinquish much of our freedom to create. Being ourselves becomes one of the purposes of creativity. Instead of trying to impress others, try to freely express yourself.

■ Be spontaneous.

We monitor our minds, just as parents regulate their children's thinking and behavior. Some of us are severe judges. Concerned about how our ideas will be received, we play it safe. Yet, too much caution ultimately works against us, because we hold back our most creative ideas for fear they will be judged harshly by others. A highly monitored child will never be truly free to play; neither will a contained mind. What if you trusted your mind's natural spontaneity and creativity?

■ Suspend judgment.

To develop playful mind, it is a good idea to suspend judgment initially so unusual ideas come quickly, including bizarre or silly ones. Sometimes, these off-the-wall ideas turn out to have hidden gems in them. Suspend judgment and watch the flow of your creative ideas increase dramatically. Afterwards, evaluate your ideas by identifying your best prospects.

■ Use imagination.

Imagine that humans had four eyes, an additional two in the back of their heads. What new idea might arise from this simple act of imagination? Could an idea be examined backwards? What new ideas would appear if, instead of thinking we have an identity, we thought backwards and declared that our identity had us? Use imagination to create surprises in the way you perceive and think. It will free your mind to play.

Freeing The Mind

When the mind is free to play, we add novel thinking, quiet chuckles, and spontaneous laughter to our lives. One way to experience this cheerful sense of freedom is to write about a topic without pausing to think.

Individual Process (10 minutes): Without lifting your pencil from the paper, write whatever comes into your mind without monitoring it. You can add punctuation, but even that is unnecessary. Topic: Write nonstop about your feet. If you want, take off your shoes and socks and explore them. Wiggle your toes. Relate to your mind as a playmate. As you write, practice the fun-da-mentals of creativity.

If you are working with a partner or group, read your work to each other. Afterwards share what it was like to practice the fun-da-mentals of creativity.

Optional Group Process (35 minutes): "Two people, one brain." This group exercise catches the mind by surprise so it produces a lot of fun and laughter. You will need at least three people. If the number of people in your group is large, divide them into groups of three. If you have an uneven number, the extra people sit out until the next round.

Set up: Decide who among the three will be the two halves of the brain. Once this is determined, those people sit or stand side-by-side facing the same direction. At no time should they look at each other. Remember, they are two halves of a single brain. The third person stands behind them. The two halves of the brain act as an expert on any topic. Together they can think about anything—the nature of the universe, love, elevators, candy, or quantum physics. The two halves of the brain, working together as an expert, cannot be wrong.

How the process works: The two halves of the brain will trust whatever comes to mind and spontaneously express it without trying to impress anyone. They will let the brain have unrestricted fun. The third person will be the hand clapper who guides the process.

Select a topic for conversation. It can be anything: "You are an expert about ears. What should we know about ears?" "You are an expert about photosynthesis. Would you please explain how that works?"

One half of the brain will start the conversation and the person standing behind will manage the conversation's flow by clapping his or her hands. The clapper should vary the time between claps and try to clap at crucial times so the brain halves are challenged to play. When the person claps, the brain half speaking stops abruptly and the other half picks up the conversation with the last word spoken. The two halves of the brain speak as one mind.

Each round should last about five to ten minutes. The clapper can determine when enough time has elapsed by noticing whether the two halves of the brain are continuing to play spontaneously. If they are, let the process continue. When the round is over, the person clapping becomes a brain half. One of the brain halves becomes the clapper. Anyone who was excluded from the round becomes a brain half, while others sit out. Before starting the next round, decide on a new topic. Then, the person clapping determines which brain half will start speaking as an expert on that topic. Following these instructions, additional rounds can be added if there is time and interest.

The value of "Two people, one brain" is that it catches the mind by surprise, so it will automatically develop new and humorous ideas. People become aware of how creative their minds are when they stop monitoring them. They are surprised by how quickly new ideas appear, some amazing in their novelty and twists of humor.

PLAYFUL MIND:
*"Silly giggles and quiet chuckles
can liberate the tightest mind."*

When the fun-da-mentals of creativity are practiced, you free the mind to play. With greater freedom, it produces a wealth of new and impressive ideas. While this is one of the purposes of cultivating playful mind, it is not its sole purpose. When playful mind ripens in you, it will permeate many aspects of your life, including your relationships, identity, and perhaps even your spirituality. Playing and laughing together with loved ones, friends, or co-workers is perhaps one of the most satisfying results of living with a more playful mind.

PLAY TIME!

Instead of using other peoples' quotes,
become the quote maker.

Meaningful quote:

Meaningless:

Outrageous:

Uplifting:

Surprising:

Funny:

Chapter 3

CLEAR INTENTIONS
INCREASE SUCCESS

I spoke with a woman recently who was passively waiting for a change to occur in her life. She was thinking the direction would appear magically.

I asked her, "What if you decided on a course? What would it be?"

"You mean, choose a direction myself? To actually take action?"

"Yes, something like that," I said. "It's called intention."

Without a clear direction, playful mind would happily frolic for months in its playground. Intention is what gives it purpose and direction. Intention is the conscious choice to define and reach a goal. When our goals are clear and we persist in achieving them, playful mind enters the adventure, helping us where it can.

Individual Process (30 minutes): What goals do you want to reach? Some near-term goals might include improving understanding with a child or mate, creating a new friendship, or adding greater vitality to your life. Record those goals on a journal page.

Circle any goal that you are determined to reach.

Select a compelling goal. What specifically will you do to reach it? Note your ideas.

If you are working with a partner or group, share your work.

Jill was teaching at a preschool when she took my creativity course. A problem preschool children face is separation from their families. It is frightening for them to experience their fears of abandonment and feel the pain of longing to be in the comforting arms of "mommy" or "daddy." Jill discovered that children can be happy one moment, remember the loss of connection to family members, then suddenly be in tears. One day, she developed a clear intention to change the situation. What she created was brilliant in its simplicity, something other teachers of young children might consider adopting.

She came up with the idea of asking the children's parents for photographs of the family, including pictures of the parents, sisters, brothers, and pets. When she had all the photographs, she cut them out and designed a small family sanctuary for the children on the wall at their eye level. Around each picture site, she glued silver glitter so the space had a special spirit. When a child began crying for mommy and daddy, she would tell the child to go have a talk with them. The child would immediately go to the family sanctuary for that talk.

Jill described how the child would speak as if the member of the family were present, then would return to normal activities feeling better. Imagine how much these children benefited from Jill's clear intention to help them. With her unique insight, she not only reduced the size of a problem faced by preschool teachers, but gave preschoolers a creative way to feel safe in a frightening situation.

Quiet Determination

Many people talk but fail to act. Some wait, hoping their dreams will come true with a stroke of luck and without effort. Creative people do not wait for luck, but move into action. Some move into such intense effort that they burn themselves out. There is a more balanced approach to success called "quiet determination." It combines the clear intention to achieve a goal with patient and steady effort. In the story of the tortoise and the hare, it is the tortoise's approach to achievement—determined and patient effort.

Using intention with quiet determination,
one hand points straight at the goal,
while the other becomes a relaxed fist of tenacity.

Balance makes things work. Striving too hard, we can inadvertently cultivate the opposition of others, make careless blunders, or lose our desire to continue. Experience this. Make a fist. Tighten it until it becomes uncomfortable. Hold it with that level of tension for a few minutes.

What do you notice? Is it difficult to maintain a sense of ease with that amount of tension? Relax your hand. Now create a loose fist of tenacity. Visualize a clear goal and forward momentum without excessive stress. Notice how easy it is to hold your hand that way. You could hold that position for a long time because your hand is in balance. Imagine pursuing your goals in that balanced way. What would change for you?

Individual Process (20 minutes): Draw a line across the center of a page. In one part, note instances where you are trying too hard and are feeling the tension of the tight fist. In the other part, record instances where you are not trying hard enough. Take an important item from each part and briefly describe what you will do to get into better balance.

If you are working with a partner or group, share what you discovered and how you are going to create more balance in your efforts.

PLAYFUL MIND:
*"When you feel yourself trying too hard,
put a little smile on your face, then relax."*

Intention and quiet determination are such simple ideas you may not fully appreciate their creative power. Together, they will help you remember where you are headed and how to get there. Instead of hurrying and risking burnout, slow down, relax, but stay determined. Over the long haul, a relaxed but determined mind has a better chance of creating good results than a tense one.

Chapter 4

Follow Your Creative Passions

What do we exclude as creative possibilities because we believe we have no talent for them? By challenging those thoughts, we can enthusiastically pursue what was rejected as a possibility. Rekindling that desire can fuel our efforts and add creative enjoyment to our lives for many years.

By considering her creative passions, Rebecca discovered that she had always wanted to make a quilt. Without hesitation, she started and became enchanted by it. At the end of the term, she proudly showed the class one large square. It was beautifully embroidered in an elaborate and original design. She promised that she would show me the quilt when it was done.

A year later, Rebecca appeared at my office door carrying a huge bundle wrapped in plastic. To my surprise and delight, she had come to show me her quilt. She carefully laid it out as I watched completely stunned. It was an exquisite work of art. Each square was beautifully embroidered with art work she had designed. The colors were amazing, bright and beautifully coordinated. Her creative passion had brought a beautiful and unique work of art into being. Happiness radiated from her. Following her creative passion, she had become a quilt artist. What she had started a year earlier had produced wonderful results.

PLAYFUL MIND:
"What you don't start, you will never finish."

Creative Possibilities

Vincent van Gogh launched his art career in his late thirties after being expelled from the church for living with the poor. He had been a Christian minister. After his expulsion, he decided to become an artist. Following that passion, he drew relentlessly. His very first drawings were beginner's sketches in terms of perspective and proportion. In his drawings of people, the heads were too large for the bodies. But he kept drawing. After countless efforts, he attained perspective and proportion. Had he responded to his first drawings with "I have no talent for this, so I'm going to give up," we would be denied the pleasure of seeing his art today.

Individual Process (25 minutes): Divide a journal page into three columns. In column one identify the things you tell yourself you cannot do: For example: "Cannot draw," "Cannot cook," "Cannot write," "Cannot use computers," "Cannot think creatively," "Cannot sew."

In column two, next to each item in column one, briefly note the story you tell yourself about why you are unable to do it.

Examine what you are sure you cannot do, but consider doing it for at least five years with the passion of Vincent van Gogh.

In the last column, enter a "Yes" next to any item you know

you could learn under those circumstances.

Make a decision. Is there something from your "Yes" list that you have a desire to start? Put a star by it.

What specific steps will you take to get started?

If you are working with a partner or group, share what you will do.

"Cannot cook" was one thing that Dana said she could not do. She realized that she was a poor cook because she never put her heart into it. "My idea of cooking has been to take the easiest route," she said. "Tuna and noodles, salad, and spaghetti have been my mainstays."

As her creative project, she decided to pursue her desire to cook. Each week, she prepared a gourmet meal for a few close friends. Before each meal, she took a photograph of it. The recipe and photograph were included in a cookbook album. As a grand finale, she prepared a gourmet meal for twenty friends. It took her several days to prepare the menu and buy the ingredients, plus hours preparing the several courses and a very elegant dessert. Her friends appeared dressed to suit the occasion. She described the night as "magical." What a change from "I cannot cook!"

*We fail to develop new talents
because we let our negative thoughts
stop us from trying.*

Start A Creative Project

Having a creative project is important because it will help you practice the creativity principles in later chapters. What you just decided to pursue by listening to your creative desire could be a project, but there are other options. You could draw, paint, sculpt, write songs, design and make clothing, take up a musical instrument, write poetry, start voice lessons, join a choir, take up quilting, or become a photographer. Creative desire may be beaconing you to start a community project to help others. The sky is the limit when it comes to what is creative, so think broadly about your choices.

If you are already deeply in a creative activity, add something new to it. If you are a composer, strike out in a different direction. If you are an architect, community organizer, painter, sculptor, dancer, fashion designer, or potter, invent a creative project that develops a unique approach within your existing work. Push through a barrier in your mind to create something new.

When exploring destinations,
include a surprising one.

Individual Process (15 minutes): On a journal page, generate as many creative ideas for projects as you can in ten minutes' time. From those, select one and briefly describe what you will do to get started. What is the first step you will take this week? If you want variety, you can try more than one project.

If you are working with a partner or group, share what you will do and when you will start. Plan a time for "show and tell" after the last chapter is completed. "Show and tell" is amazing, moving, and fun. Invite friends to join you. Make it into a celebration.

Motivated by a desire to write, Jenny's creative project was to capture in prose what she had learned from her five sisters. Her writing was to be an acknowledgment of them for what they had given her. She also wanted to convey the essence of what she had given them, but could not find an appropriate way.

As she spoke about this dilemma, it became clear that her effort was only marginally about writing. The real objective was to express and deepen love. With love in mind, she decided to bring her sisters together at Christmas time to read what she had written. Then she would ask each sister to spend time sharing what she had learned from the others. What her sisters learned from her would emerge as they revealed important emotional connections. She hoped that an occasion of such deep sharing would create more love between them and build a foundation for deepening their relationships.

She carried out her project over the Christmas holidays. When she returned, she shared the love that was created. "An amazing and beautiful experience," she said, "definitely something others should try."

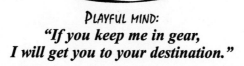

PLAYFUL MIND:
"If you keep me in gear,
I will get you to your destination."

As you make your way through this book, you may find yourself wanting to create things that nourish your creativity, like making your own greeting cards or adding a creativity space in your home. Following those impulses is part of adding creativity to different parts of your life. Have fun creating wherever you want. Bring friends and family into it as well. Soon, those around you will be cultivating playful mind and more creative lives.

On an impulse, Lindsey decided to create a deeper feeling of community with her friends. She invited three friends to join her in adding art work to a wooden kitchen table. Each took up a corner of the table and painted spontaneously, paying careful attention to how the separate works would be integrated into a pleasing whole. They made up quotes to add at the end. Not only did they create a unique work of art, but they loved doing it together. This deepened their friendship.

Terri was part of a Thursday night bar hopping group until she got the bright idea to convert it into "Creativity Night." Instead of drinking, she and her friends carried out creative activities together and loved it.

Adding creative adventures like these to your larger project will help you live the creative life more fully.

Chapter 5

You Are Gifted

*M*any of us have an easy time noticing other peoples' talents, but fail to appreciate our own. When asked to focus on our own gifts, we discover important ones: The gifts of courage, perseverance, planning, leadership, or the ability to solve problems in novel ways. Maybe we have the capacity to inspire others. Being clear about our gifts and knowing that we can create new resources strengthens our creativity. Our gifts are the personal resources we use to create good relationships, invent rituals, design and build houses, solve problems, write books, create new ideas, or make up songs to sing to a child falling asleep in our arms.

Typically someone will say at this point: "Yes, humans are resourceful, but not me." Josh put it cryptically: "My creativity tool box is nearly empty." After doing the following work, people learn that their creativity tool boxes are full enough for living a more creative life.

With a few essential tools,
you can build a house.
With a few essential resources,
you can live more creatively.

Recovering Creativity From Your Childhood

Spend one hour with a seven-year-old child and it becomes apparent that creativity and children go hand-in-hand. Children can play for hours, their imaginations alive and active, not knowing where the time went. In fact, they forget about time. They become so fully absorbed in play, it becomes real to them. "Let's pretend" loses its imaginary quality once the action starts. The boundary between imagination and reality is much less distinct for them than adults, who know they are pretending.

When I talk to people about creativity, I discover a fair number who are reluctant to try anything creative. They dried up early. Their creativity spigot was turned off. It is "premature aging of the mind."

No one can stop your creativity
as fast as you can.

We are naturally creative as children but lose some of it because of what others say to us and what we come to believe about ourselves. Yet, what we have lost can be reclaimed. In the following work, you will go into the past to recover what you left behind.

Individual Process (30 minutes): Remember what it felt like to be about 7 years old. If that was a difficult time in your life, go to an age when things were better and your creativity was alive and vital.

As that age, notice how you were naturally creative in play. Recall an attitude you had then that supported your creativity that was lost or diminished in power through years of education. Perhaps it was the freedom to try things or a willingness to take risks. Close your eyes and let your mind focus on the attitudes in childhood that made you creative. Choose at least one gift to bring back into the present.

Now, remember your favorite toy or game as a child. Close your eyes. Watch yourself using that toy or playing that game. What creative abilities did that toy or game bring out in you? Imagination? Spontaneity? Be ready to bring back those abilities into your current life.

Return with the attitudes and abilities that supported your creativity in childhood.

If you are working with a partner or group, share the gifts you brought back. Talk about your favorite toy and what creative abilities it cultivated in you.

When you want to be creative, use the abilities inspired by your favorite toy or game. If one was imagination, then use it often. It will naturally work for you. My favorite toy as a child was dirt. I loved it. Dirt was fun because it called upon my ability to improvise. When I honor that ability to improvise today, my creativity emerges naturally.

Individual Process (30 minutes): Begin by tearing a sheet of paper into small pieces. Write the gifts you brought back from your childhood on separate slips.

Think about the other creative gifts you have. Write those gifts on separate slips.

Create a circular pattern with your most important gifts in the middle.

On separate slips, note the gifts that you have not fully

acknowledged. Maybe you have not recognized your ability to listen carefully or to complete tasks on time. Stretch your mind to discover your unrecognized gifts. Add those to the pattern where they belong.

Next, note gifts you could develop if you committed yourself to cultivating them. Add those to your pattern. Is one a potentially important gift that should be placed toward the center?

Recess of the mind: Contemplate the pattern of your gifts. What do you notice?

If you are working with a partner or group, share your insights.

Now that you are more aware of your gifts:

Which ones will you emphasize in order to develop more creativity in your life?

How will you use your gifts?

PLAYFUL MIND:
*"What gifts could you adopt
from your favorite pet?"*

Individual Process (5 minutes): Write down four words that come to mind when you think about your personal gifts.

Use the words in a poem to express your creative potential.

If you are working with a partner or group, read your poems to each other.

Sandy was a well-known community organizer when she took one of my creativity workshops. She had a distinguished record of community service stretching back for years and had created highly successful community programs. Even with her amazing achievements, she had no clear sense of her gifts before she did this work. If anything, she diminished her importance as an agent of social change. After becoming aware of her gifts, she said with surprise, "Hey, I guess I do have some important gifts." By realizing her gifts, she became aware of her unique contribution. She could also see more clearly where her gifts could be used to serve others.

Chapter 6

TAKE RISKS

I can still recall the countless hours I spent working in coloring books as a child. In school, I learned to color inside the lines and was applauded by my teacher when I succeeded. If I was careless and accidentally strayed outside a line, I felt the whole page was ruined and threw it away before my teacher saw it. When I succeeded in completing a page with the colors neatly and fully within the lines, I showed my work with pride. Through that simple coloring exercise, I learned to get praise by conforming and playing it safe.

There are people who will insist that we think and behave inside the lines. Sometimes we can resist and go our own way. At other times, we have no option but conformity.

Individual Process (15 minutes): Where in your life are you being required or pressured to live inside the lines? What are you unable to try? How does the confinement make you feel? Note your answers in your journal.

Where are you asking others to live inside the lines? What are they unable to try? How does it make them feel? Add brief answers to these questions.

If you are working with a partner or group, share the insights that emerged from your writing.

*People will want you to live in
the same-sized mind boxes that they live in.*

Conventional people live in conventional-sized mind boxes and develop rationalizations about why it is preferable to live that way. Sometimes the rationalization develops into orthodoxy. As active thought guardians, they see their job as upholding the norms and values of the group. They will resist anything that might lead the group off course, threaten its standards, or undermine its morality.

Unlike the guardians, creators question the way things are done. While orthodox guardians try to keep things settled, creators stir things up and seek change. They challenge existing knowledge or methods to cause breakthroughs. Howard Gardner chronicles this independent spirit in the lives of Freud, Einstein, Picasso, Stravinsky, Eliot, Graham, and Gandhi in his book *Creating Minds*. Reading about the lives of these gifted people, one is struck by their brashness, even ego inflation. When the creative spirit exists outside of an established group, strong individualism of this kind can produce great breakthroughs in thinking, technique, design, and action.

In groups, guardians and creators can turn into trouble makers if they become too rigid and extreme. If guardians are too conventional, they can block the flow of creative ideas, which undermines the ability of the group to thrive in a changing environment. If creators are too radical, they can alienate the guardians to the point where a great deal of time and energy is wasted on conflict resolution. When the guardians and creators are flexible and cooperative, they balance each others' tendencies, which can produce healthy cross-currents of stability and innovation.

How to confuse the guardians:
Avoid blue hair, and nose, tongue,
and multiple ear piercing.
Instead of trying to look creative,
just be creative.
Look normal and you will
get away with a lot.

Be Prepared For Dream Wreckers

When pursuing creative interests, we face many obstacles. A major one is the active discouragement and resistance of others, people who revel in explaining why our dream is a bad idea or beyond our reach. While being receptive to feedback from others is a good idea, it is important to avoid people who enjoy undermining the hopes of others. Armed with strong opinions, pessimism, cynicism, or envy, these "dream wreckers" may be friends, teachers, sisters, brothers, parents, or strangers who become vociferous predictors of doom.

David dreamt of becoming a musician. I had seen him perform, so I knew he was a talented singer, guitarist, and song writer. When I mentioned his musical aspirations to his father, he laughed. Choosing a mocking tone, his words were biting: "Be real. That's such a long shot it's not going to happen and, if it does, it will be a marginal life with few monetary rewards."

Pain and disappointment crossed David's face as he turned away from his father. He said nothing, but his expression quietly apologized for his father's lack of support and callousness. He shrugged his shoulders with regret. Someone

37

important in his life had undermined his dream and crushed his spirit. It was a tense and sad moment.

Think of the people who actively discourage you from pursuing your dreams. They may call your dreams "fantasies," while wanting to say "Get real." It takes courage to stand up to these "crazy makers," as Julia Cameron calls them in *The Artist's Way*. Holding a superior attitude, they become harsh critics who see only what is wrong with us and our work.

On occasion, I hear about professors who are so severe in criticizing students it borders on abuse. A bright, young student of mine was in tears after being harshly criticized by a professor for a paper she had written. The professor is notorious among students in his department. They know he cherishes the few students he feels worthy of his attention, while he undermines the rest. He told her the paper was worthless, written like a juvenile, and he did not want her in his class. She asked if he would help her to improve her writing. He flatly refused, saying her writing was "hopeless." After dropping his class and enrolling in the course of a graduate student teacher who willingly helped her, her writing improved.

Individual Process (20 minutes): On a journal page, record the judgments of others that undermined your creativity. Instead of thinking what they said was true, develop your own judgment. Try the following responses for practice.

■ "You could be wrong."
■ "I will assume you are wrong."

Describe two other ways you could respond to your judges.

Now, read one of those judgments aloud, then select a

response to it, speaking to the person as if he or she were sitting across from you. Repeat this process for each judgment. Experience your ability to stop the judgments of others from stopping you.

Recess of the mind: Take a few minutes to reflect on what you learned.

If you are working with a partner or group, share your discoveries.

Additional Group Process (10 minutes): Work with a partner. Exchange what you have written about the judgments of others. Take turns reading one of the judgments leveled against your partner, then listen to your partner's respond to the judgment. When all critics have been put in their place, discuss how you will deal with dream wreckers in the future.

You are cultivating the capacity to maintain your creative momentum in the face of other peoples' resistance. Unlike good coaches who will want to help you achieve your goals, "dream wreckers" will try to convince you not to start, will undermine your confidence if you do, and will encourage you to give up along the way. When you are able to pursue your dreams in the face of that resistance, you claim the right to have the life you want. It is a declaration that you are a creative person who cannot be stopped.

PLAYFUL MIND:
*"Imagine that you have the power of a bulldozer
to clear away any obstacles in your path."*

Anne had always wanted to play the flute, but her parents

strongly discouraged her, telling her that music was not her forte. She accepted their judgment and omitted music from her life. When she entered my creativity class, she spoke to me about her strong desire to play the flute. I asked her what was stopping her from finding a teacher and starting lessons.

"When I was young my parents discouraged me from pursuing music," she said.

"What if you questioned their judgment? What if they were wrong? In fact, let's say they were wrong. What would it take for you to get started?"

After pausing for a moment, she responded. "I'd have to find a flute teacher, then find a flute somewhere, because I have no money to buy one."

"Okay," I said, "find the teacher."

Within a week, she came to me with the news that she had found a teacher. "Good, now I will supply the flute," I said. The following week she broke into a big smile when I handed her a flute I had stopped playing. "It's a loan until you reach a point where you want and can afford a flute of your own." "It's a deal," she said before thanking me.

Her musical training began the next week. She loved it and practiced with a deep commitment because her desire to play the flute was so strong.

Two years later, Anne came by my office to return the flute. She had bought a much higher quality flute of her own and was so accomplished that she could play with skill and enjoyment. By saying "No" to her parents' judgment, she said "Yes" to her creative desire.

A NOTE TO PARENTS, TEACHERS, SPOUSES, AND FRIENDS:
Watch what you say.
You can inadvertently stop
the creative flow of a person's life.

Getting Out Of "Thinking Traps"

Guardians pressure us to play it safe and dream wreckers discourage us, but we can also create our own "Thinking Traps." A "Thinking Trap" is made up of beliefs that confine our thinking. It is a mind box that prevents us from discovering new ideas and approaches.

Individual Process (20 minutes): To understand how a Thinking Trap is constructed, draw a large box on a journal page to represent a trap. Divide it into four boxes. Choose an issue to explore. It might be personal, a relationship problem, or a project that needs new inspiration and vitality.

Realize that you have created your own thinking trap. Write your responses to each of the following questions, taking them one at a time and recording your ideas in one of the four boxes.

What ideas have you:

■ Excluded from consideration because of your beliefs? Note those in a box.

■ Banned because of your awareness about how the issue was approached in the past? Note those in another box.

■ Omitted because they seem too risky? Note them in a third box.

- Not allowed yourself to imagine? Record them in the final box.

Next, identify your best prospects by putting a circle around them. Put stars by your two leading ideas.

Using those two ideas, develop a new approach to your issue.

If you are working with a partner or group, share what you created.

PLAYFUL MIND:
"Where you feel confined, think 'escape'."

Today, creativity is fast becoming a part of the language of organizations as they adapt to the speeding tempo of change and try to solve difficult problems. More than ever, there are opportunities for people who know they are creative and who welcome the chance to be imaginative and far-reaching in their thinking.

When my students are looking for jobs, I encourage them to put their creativity in the center of any interview. Molly did this recently. She described starting her interview by first explaining that she was a creative person who welcomed creative challenges. While she talked about creativity, her enthusiasm rose dramatically. Due to her enthusiasm, she received many positive comments from the interviewers at the end. She also got the job.

PLAY TIME!

Color outside the lines!

Use outlandish colors!

Chapter 7

Small Changes Can Produce Big Results

There are times when a major change can be productive, but the power of small changes should not be overlooked. Changes begun with the idea of sweeping, dramatic results can move people out of balance and into more chaos than they can handle productively, whereas the idea of a "minor remodel" is modest and emphasizes the concepts of "gradual" and "patient." If we are prepared for chaos, then transformation may work; if not, undertaking a modest remodel is a good idea.

Playful Mind:
"Add a little window to your mind.
How would that little alteration change you?"

Individual Process (20 minutes): In the following work, you will apply "Simple math: Subtract one thing, add one thing." This technique is based loosely on fractal theory in physics, which suggests that if you alter one thing slightly, larger changes will occur over time.

At the top of a journal page, record things you would like to change or projects that need new ideas. Select one to work on.

Divide the remaining part of the page in half. In one half, identify two things you could add to what you are doing that might make a difference. This could include changes within yourself. Circle your best prospect.

In the other half, indicate two things that you could subtract from what you are doing that could make a nice difference. Circle your best prospect.

Using your best ideas, develop a strategy for change.

If you are working with a partner or group, share your results.

Small changes can produce big results. A manager who wanted to change how she felt about her work subtracted one small thing that made a big difference. She called her staff together and announced that she would no longer gossip about anyone in the group. This subtraction made her feel more positive about herself and her group, and it inspired another person to quit gossiping. By applying the principle of "Simple Math," she made a change that could influence the course of her organization in major ways over the next few years. Imagine an organization where gossip never occurs. What could that organization achieve from that one change alone?

What Are Your Life Purposes?

One small thing that can be added to our thinking are our life purposes. When we are clear about our purposes, it is easier to know what to create in our lives. Knowledge of our life purposes helps us discriminate between what is important and insignificant. Among all the requests for our time, energy, and money, suddenly we know which ones to accept and decline.

Individual Process: (25 minutes): In the middle of a journal page, put "My life purposes." For five minutes, let your mind play with the question: "What are the purposes I want my life to serve?" Note your ideas. Some life purposes may be directed toward serving others, some toward taking care of yourself. Consider both realms.

Stretch your thinking. Make up two purposes you have not allowed yourself to imagine and add them to your work.

Circle four purposes you want you life to serve.

What path are those purposes encouraging you to take? Write a brief letter to yourself as if your purposes were guiding you. In your letter, describe a mission for your life that your creativity will serve.

If you are working with a partner or group, share your letters and discoveries.

When your life purposes are clear, you will have a better understanding about how to shape and focus your creativity to realize your life's mission. At that moment, your creativity becomes a tool for cultivating a life of deeper meaning.

Chapter 8

MANAGING YOUR FEARS

When I attended an art exhibit of a friend, her best friend Nancy took me on a tour, telling me in an animated way about the art. It was obvious that Nancy had a passion for art, but had been unwilling to take the risk of becoming an artist herself. She advised my artist friend and basked in reflected glory.

When there was a pause in the conversation, I saw my opportunity: "You have a love for art," I said. "When are you going to start?" She quickly admitted that she had been wanting to do art for a long time, but held back.

A few days later when I was on the phone with my friend, I asked if Nancy had started some art of her own. "No, she said she isn't ready yet."

"She's afraid" was my reply. "Yes," my friend responded.

The prospect of becoming more creative may be scary because there is an element of risk. If Nancy could admit her fear rather than believe she is not quite ready, she could take steps to add art to her life. When we know what is frightening about creativity, we have a better chance of managing our fears. When we are unaware, the fears are likely to control us and limit what we undertake.

Individual Process (15 minutes): At the top of a journal page, put "Fears I have about becoming more creative." Indicate any fears you have about expanding your creativity. For example, Nancy was probably afraid that she did not have enough talent to succeed as an artist.

As you note a fear, be aware that it is a thought you believe is true. Consider that it might not be.

If you think you have no imagination,
look at your fears.

Managing Your Ego Size

Children in the early years of elementary school seem comfortable with creativity. Yet they become more afraid of it as they age. Some adults who are afraid of creativity have forgotten that they did not fear it as children.

Recess of the mind: Let your mind focus on the questions: What made you less afraid of creativity as a child? What makes you more afraid now?

Young children have not yet learned to feel inadequate, unless their parents embedded the idea early. As children develop, they learn to feel deficient in knowledge, skills, social graces, and personality. As children learn to feel deficient, they become more self-conscious. They reveal anxiety about their social performance and presentation of self. Feelings of inadequacy are heightened by failure, other peoples' criticisms, and the negative judgments they learn to hold about themselves. Not wanting to feel incompetent, they become conscious of a need to manage the size of their egos. They learn to avoid circumstances that deflate their egos because that makes them feel bad, while they pursue opportunities to shine so their egos can feel big and good. Almost everyone becomes tarnished by inadequacy in this way. Most of us spend considerable effort trying to manage the size of our egos each day.

Observe yourself carefully for one day. Notice how much time and energy you invest in keeping your ego at a reasonable size.

What do you do to feel big and good?
What do you do to avoid feeling little and bad?

Nancy was managing the size of her ego when she delayed becoming an artist. She avoided the risk of feeling little and miserable if she failed. She felt bigger and better in the illusion that she was a hidden artist. By deciding she was not ready to pursue art, she preserved her ego's size but sacrificed the adventure of art.

Individual Process (20 minutes): On a journal page, indicate what your ego wants from creativity. Perhaps it wants to impress others, be challenged, feel superior, or have a good time. When you are finished, circle needs where it is clear your ego is trying to compensate for your feelings of inadequacy.

Next to the needs you circled, identify a fear that emerges from them. For instance, if your ego wants acclaim, you might fear being unknown.

What are your insights?

If you are working with a partner or group, share what you

learned.

Instead of creativity being an opportunity for fun and a great challenge, it can become another "proving ground." Concerned that our creative efforts receive public praise, our freedom to create can quickly be replaced by the desire to cater to the whims of others. Instead of seeing creativity as the need to prove ourselves, we can simply share what we create. Instead of focusing on results, we can enter into the adventure and deep enjoyment of the creative process. Approaching creativity this way allows creative energy to flow more freely within us. When we get our egos out of the way, our minds will naturally want to play.

Through this shift in thinking, we reclaim what children have which makes them innovators. With less ego, they engage in creativity for the fun and excitement of it. They are not trying to get anything or prove anything; they love the process. Remember the countless hours, even days, you spent in imaginary games with your friends as a child? What if you had that capacity to get completely absorbed in the creative process now?

The freedom to create is achieved the moment we quit using creativity to prove our worth to others.

Individual Process (10 minutes): Practice putting your ego to sleep. Write a short poem about your teeth or nose. Establish the goal of having fun rather than trying to prove yourself. If you are working alone, read it to a friend later. Share what you learned about ego, fear, and the freedom to create.

If you are working with a partner or group, read your poems to each other. As you prepare to read your work, notice if fear emerges and wonder why.

Fear does not go away, but it can be managed so we are not immobilized by it. If we waited for fear to disappear, we might postpone taking action indefinitely. By calling upon our courage to take a risk, we add the excitement of pursuing our own ideas. By avoiding wild risks, we reduce the size of our fears. We learn to live in balance but on the creative edge. We are living on the edge when we can take risks but not such large ones that we are overcome with anxiety.

By balancing adventure and security,
we experience mild perspiration,
not heavy sweating.

Contemplate your fears about creativity and your capacity to take risks:

Where are you playing it too safe?
Where are you too reckless?

Remember a time when you lived on the edge—when you took a risk but also felt a sense of safety. What did that experience produce?

PLAYFUL MIND:
"Risk is the willingness to discover
if something new is possible."

By taking risks, you will add more adventure to your life. Sharon discovered this. She was attracted to a shy man who held back from asking her out. She imagined herself making a sign that she would hand to him. It said: "Take a break from being shy and take a chance with me." This gave her the courage to take the initiative. She said: "I realized that I could ask him out. I didn't need to give him the risk and all the power." He was happy she asked. Now, they are a couple in a great relationship. This would not have happened if Sharon had been unwilling to take a risk. By escaping the limitations imposed on her thinking by society and choosing to try a new approach, she created something of great value.

Chapter 9

YOU CAN CREATE INSPIRATION

Some of us fall into creativity ruts when inspiration fails us. We wait for the creative Muse to inspire us, hoping for an unexpected insight or an image for a painting or story to appear spontaneously in a dream. Such moments of inspiration should be prized, but there is no need to wait for them. They can be created by arbitrarily choosing an inspiration point to enliven our thinking about any topic. For example, we can establish "freedom," "courage," "fun," or "spiritual" as inspiration points. Bringing nature to mind, maybe we try "sky," "water," "mud," or "earthquake."

Using inspiration points quickly alters our point of view so new ideas begin appearing as if by magic. Imagine starting a creative project by letting your mind first play with the inspiration point "lightening." Then, notice how your mind would create different ideas if you started with "love."

THE CREATIVE MUSE SPEAKS:
*"Will you please wake up and
create your own inspiration?
Frankly, I'm tired of you depending on me
and then whining when I'm silent."*

Individual Process (30 minutes): In the middle of a page, indicate an issue that you would like to explore. It might be something you need to create at work or school, in the art realm, or in a relationship. Divide the page into four parts. Without thinking too much, create an inspiration point in each part. Maybe the first word that comes into your mind is "water." Use it as an inspiration point. Imagine how playing off the word "water" will inspire the appearance of unusual ideas.

With your inspiration points in place, begin spontaneously jotting down ideas in each part, letting the uniqueness of each inspiration point kindle its own creative fire. You can focus your work in one part or shift back and forth between them.

Next, circle ideas that seem worth pursuing.

Take one and briefly lay out a plan of action.

Recess of the mind: Focus on your ability to create your own inspiration. How will you use it?

If you are working with a partner or group, share your discoveries.

PLAYFUL MIND:
*"Inspiration is the spark you make
to get your creative fire going."*

I know a gifted painter. His work is realistic and his technique is impressive. One day I asked him what inspiration point he painted from. He was unable to grasp the meaning of my question until I explained the concept of inspiration points. Without further prompting, he then realized that his inspiration point had always been to "make the painting look like the object being observed." His work was nourished by this inspiration for realism, but it caused his paintings to be too carefully crafted. He knew this and was seeking a change because he had lost his enthusiasm for art.

I asked him what new inspiration point he would like to establish. "Fun," he said without pausing. Using fun as his new inspiration point felt awkward to him at first because it put him in unknown territory. Yet, as he played and took new risks, his style became more open and spontaneous. Eventually he achieved a nice balance between loose and tight that transformed his work, not only in the spontaneity of his design and brush work, but in his more courageous use of color. By altering his inspiration point, he enhanced the quality and power of his art.

What areas of your life could be altered by a simple change of inspiration point?

What inspiration point would you use?

What new ideas for change would it awaken in you?

> THE CREATIVE MUSE SPEAKS AGAIN:
> *"Finally, you understand how*
> *to create your own inspiration.*
> *What a relief!*
> *Now, I can do something else."*

Chapter 10

USE IMAGINATION
TO FREE YOUR MIND

*C*reating inspiration points is a step toward cultivating a richer imagination. By its very nature, imagination loosens rigid categories and ways of perceiving so new ideas come quickly. An ability to imagine can be used to restore creativity when we feel stuck or have convinced ourselves we have nothing to say. In teaching, there are times when someone will respond to a question by saying: "I don't know what to say about that." Aware of the power of imagination, I will respond: "Well, imagine that you know." This simple shift to imagination has a magical effect because the student begins generating ideas.

Three creative techniques will be introduced to expand our imagination: "Pretend!," "What if?," and "Future Stretch." They are easy and fun to use and produce immediate results.

PLAYFUL MIND:
*"Imagine that you are an artist with a
full palette of colors who can't wait to get started.
Imagine that you are the colors longing to be used."*

Pretend!

"Let's pretend" is a child's way of introducing imagination into play. As adults, many of us lose that ability to pretend. Like a muscle that atrophies from lack of use, the mind quits being as playful if we rarely use our imaginations. Restoring imagination is crucial for expanding creativity in our lives because of its remarkable power to awaken playful mind. As a creative technique, "Pretend!" establishes imagination as a creativity tool.

Individual Process (20 minutes): Pretend you have contact with a wise being on another planet in our galaxy whose name is Togi. Close your eyes. In your imagination, have a conversation with Togi in which you ask any question and Togi will answer with wisdom. Record what Togi says in your journal.

If you are working with a partner or group, share what you learned from Togi.

TWO FIVE-YEAR-OLD GIRLS:
(First girl) "Let's pretend to be serious and uptight."
(Second girl) "Oh, good, we get to play grown ups!"

What if?

By asking the question "What if?", we encourage imagination and our ability to pretend. What if there were playgrounds for adults? What if the experience of obligation did not exist? What if we could feel each other's joy? What if we could think about a problem with the mind of a five year-old child? Anytime a breakthrough in thinking is needed, we ask "What if?" It is a question that will help us dream up unusual possibilities.

Individual Process (20 minutes): Identify a situation in your life where you feel frustrated, stuck, or stagnant and record it in the middle of a page. Using imagination, jot down all the "What if?" questions about that situation that come to mind. For example, suppose you are uncertain about how to approach your boss to ask for a raise. Some "What if" questions: What if I assumed my boss will say 'Yes' with enthusiasm? What if I thought "award" rather than raise? (What should I be getting an award for?) What if my boss were asking me for a raise? (How would she ask?)

After laying out your "What if?' questions, circle your most promising ideas for change.

Where do you see an opening for change?
A path to explore?
Something to try?

If you are working with a partner or group, reveal what you learned.

---

*What if you put play into business
and business into play?*

Future Stretch

Knowledge of the past and present limit what we are able to imagine. For example, if we were designing a new children's park, we would recall children's parks from the past and recall how they are currently designed. The range and novelty of our ideas would be restricted by what we already know. A "future stretch" takes our attention off the past and present by transporting us to a time far in the future. Unable to rely on what is known, our imagination takes over.

Individual Process (20 minutes): In two hundred years, people will be cleaning their teeth in an entirely different way. Invent ideas for the product that was developed.

Enter your ideas and a rough design of the product in your journal.

If you are working with a partner or group, co-create ideas, then design the new product together. If you are working in a large group, divide into smaller groups. Share your designs with each other, followed by discussion.

Anytime a problem or project needs playful mind, turn to imagination and the specific techniques of pretending, asking "what if?" questions, and future stretches. They will add surprises to your thinking.

PLAYFUL MIND:
"What if your mind was a children's story book,
a runaway train, a flashing light, or an empty can?"

PLAY TIME!

Draw yourself as a cartoon character.
Put words in your mouth.

Chapter 11

SHIFT PERSPECTIVES
TO CREATE NEW IDEAS

Sometimes our mind is made up and we resist disturbing its sense of certainty. At those times, shifting perspectives can do us a world of good. By taking a different point of view, we quickly see any issue in a new light. "Mind Switching" generates new ideas by pulling us out of our comfortable perspectives and into the minds of others. "Roleing Around" helps us explore new ideas by thinking from a different social role.

MIND-SWITCHING BUMPER STICKER:
"Would your mother be tailgating me?"

Individual Process (25 minutes): When designing a project or new solutions to a problem, use Mind Switching to explore the thinking of a person who could add new insights to your work.

In your journal, identify issues where you would benefit from a shift of perspective. Then, select an issue for Mind Switching.

Identify people whose perspectives might be helpful to you, whose point of view you value or whose ideas are different from yours. Former teachers who influenced you, friends, or public figures are possibilities. Circle the name of the person whose mind you most want to visit.

Sit with your eyes closed. Imagine yourself being able to think with that person's mind.

How would that person think about your issue?
How would your issue be approached and analyzed?
What novel ideas might surface within that person's mind?

When the mind visit is over, record your insights. How did your mind visit shift your perspective? What novel ideas or options do you see now?

If you are working with a partner or group, share what you learned.

An additional opportunity: If the individual whose mind you visited is someone you know, consider setting up a meeting to directly probe that person's thinking about your issue. Intend to leave the conversation with a change of perspective and new ideas.

PLAYFUL MIND:
"Everyone's mind is a library open to visitors."

"Roleing Around"

Another interesting and entertaining way of creating new ideas is to take the perspective of a person in a different social role. What could I learn from a brain surgeon about my issue? A mortician? A police officer? A professional photographer? A mother? "Roleing Around" is a creative technique for shifting perspectives by taking on different social roles. It helps expand what we see. New and sometimes surprising ideas come with little effort.

PLAYFUL MIND:
"What can a clown learn from a physicist about clowning? What can a physicist learn from a clown about black holes?"

Individual Process (30 minutes): Decide on an issue to address. Maybe you want to develop new ideas for vacations, design an alternative school, or create novel ways of having fun. Note the issue in the middle of a page.

Tear up a piece of paper into six parts. On each slip, quickly record a social role. Perhaps the first that come to mind are "Teacher, child, stock broker, minister, gardener, and basketball player." Place them face down and mix them.

Choose a role. Put yourself in that role and allow new and unusual ideas to appear. How would the person in that role think about your issue? Jot down your ideas.

When you need to renew playful mind, select another role and generate creative ideas by taking on that role. Add those ideas to your work.

Take a third role and repeat the idea-generating process.

When you have done enough Roleing Around, circle your most promising ideas. Take one and describe how you will implement it. What first steps will you take?

If you are working with a partner or group, share your work.

Optional Group Process (50 minutes): If your group is large, divide into small groups of about four people.

Decide on the focus of the group's effort. Is there a project to design? A communication problem to solve?

Tear a piece of paper into six parts. Together, decide on social roles that someone records on the slips. Place the roles face down and mix them. Have someone randomly select a role. Taking on that role together, co-create new ideas about your issue. Someone in the group records the ideas.

When the group needs new inspiration, another role is chosen and the process is repeated.

Take a third role and shift your perspective again.

Circle your most promising ideas, then formulate a plan of action together. If you are part of a large group, reconvene to share your work.

A computer designer was struggling with the problem of how to create a keyboard for a very small laptop that was large enough so it was comfortable to use. One day, a creative thought occurred to him: "How would my five year-old son think about this?" He remembered how much his son loved to build with blocks. This inspired the man to design a keyboard that divided in half when the computer was being closed. To fit inside the computer case, one half of the keyboard was stacked like a block on top of the other.

Look For Hidden Gems

When our minds are playing, outrageous ideas will spontaneously occur to us. During evaluation, when choosing our most promising ideas, they are usually discarded. Without knowing it, "hidden gems" are lost, ideas that seem outlandish on the surface until they are mined carefully. Then, their value is revealed.

At a paint manufacturing company an employee said as a joke, "Let's add gunpowder to paint so it can be blown off when people are ready to repaint." Seeing the possibility of a hidden gem in this comment, more constructive options emerged for removing paint quickly and efficiently. The result was a new product, sheets of chemically treated material that can be placed over a painted surface. The chemicals in the material interact with the chemicals in the paint, so the paint lifts from the surface when the sheets are removed. By taking a joke and mining it for a new idea, a useful product was invented.

PLAYFUL MIND:
"Would you please start a recycling program for your thinking waste?"

Individual or Group Process (20 minutes): Whether working alone or in a group, go back to the ideas you developed while "Roleing Around." Circle the far-fetched ones you discarded and select one to mine. Produce a workable idea from it. If you are working alone, jot down ideas in your journal. If you are working with a group, co-create ideas. Report your results if you are part of a larger group.

Think of the ways that shifting perspectives can help you create new ideas.

What new ideas for home construction might emerge by visiting the brain of a bee?

What could a comedian teach you about designing a new home?

Chapter 12

QUESTION YOUR ASSUMPTIONS

"*B*reak out!" is a creative technique for challenging our assumptions in order to transform our rigid thinking. Assumptions are beliefs that we are convinced are true, so we no longer notice or question them. They operate in the background and restrict what we are able to perceive and think. They are like invisible bars of a cell that imprison our minds. To free ourselves, we have to clearly understand the assumptions that are confining our thinking, then challenge them. If we want to experience an expansion of perspective about any topic, we first identify and challenge our assumptions, then notice how quickly our minds begin to play. Refreshing new ideas appear the moment we question our taken-for-granted beliefs.

BUMPER STICKER:
"The Truth is where we have quit thinking."

Individual Process: (20 minutes): On a journal page, note a few situations or problems where creative thinking could make a difference. It might be something you have given up trying to resolve even though it could be changed. Maybe it is a project that is going nowhere. It could be an important relationship where adding creativity could help to enliven it.

Once you have developed some options, choose one issue to work on.

For five minutes, note all the assumptions you have about it. What are the beliefs about the issue you are assuming to be true? Notice those as limitations you place on your own thinking.

Identify your four most limiting assumptions. Those are the main bars of your thinking prison. Circle the assumption that confines your thinking most profoundly.

To create new ideas for change, you will "Run the Bases." It is a technique that will require you to invent four new ideas about any issue.

In your journal, draw a baseball diamond with first base, second, third, and home. In the middle, write the assumption that most profoundly limits your thinking.

Cross out the assumption. As you do, feel yourself rejecting it.

Having rejected the assumption, what new creative possibilities do you see? Run the bases, offering an option for change at each base. Create a surprising idea when you reach home base.

When you finish running the bases, take a few minutes to review your options. Circle your most promising one.

Develop a plan of action to implement that idea. What first step will you take? When?

If you are working with a partner or group, share what you are planning to do.

Break Out! Applied to an Organization

Break Out! can change how we view yourselves, our roles, our power, and how we perceive an organization where we spend time. It could be our workplace, a nonprofit corporation where we do community service, or a college we attend. It might be a religious organization, a social club, or our family. After becoming aware of the assumptions that limit our thinking, we "run the bases" to create four novel ideas for initiating a change.

Individual Process (30 minutes): Decide which organization will be the focus of your work.

At the top of a journal page, indicate the organization you have chosen. Beneath it, make four large squares to represent prison cells.

Above each cell, write one of the following statements:

> "My self: Assumptions I hold about
> my self in the organization;"

> "My role: Assumptions I hold about
> my role in the organization;"

> "My power: Assumptions I hold about
> my power in the organization;"

> "The Organization: Assumptions I hold about
> the organization."

The work you will do in each cell will make you more aware of hidden beliefs that have been restricting your thinking.

My self. What assumptions do you hold and never question about your self in the organization? Note those in the cell.

My role. What assumptions do you hold and never question about your role in the organization? Record those.

My power. What assumptions do you hold and never question about your power in the organization? Note them.

The organization. What assumptions do you hold and never question about the organization? Record them.

Circle your most limiting assumption in each cell.

Identify the most limiting one from among those.

Draw a baseball diamond on a page in your journal with first base, second, third, and home. In the middle, write your most limiting assumption.

Reject it by crossing it out. Feel the freedom to generate new options in your thinking.

Run the bases. When you get to first, note a new idea for making a change. Go to second, note another one. When you touch third, identify an unusual option. When you reach home, come up with a surprising possibility.

Take your most promising idea and develop a brief plan to implement it. What is one thing you could do this week to move into action?

Recess of the mind: Contemplate your work. What insights are emerging? Where are you noticing break outs in your thinking? What other limiting assumptions would you like to challenge and change by running the bases?

If you are working with a partner or group, share what you discovered.

SCRAWLED IN THE MARGIN OF A BOOK:
"If you want to transform your thinking, challenge what you are already sure is true."

Assumptions are like lines in a coloring book that stop us from seeing new possibilities. They trap our thinking in convention. Unaware of their hidden influence, we may be absolutely certain that what we are doing is the only way to do it. Children can sometimes awaken us to a different reality. Tiffany learned this from Kip, a five-year-old boy she was caring for as a nanny.

Tiffany picked up Kip from school. When she saw him, she was shocked to discover that he was wearing a pajama top as an undershirt. In a disappointed and judging tone, she said with emphasis, "What are you wearing?" Looking quite proud, Kip responded, "I'm wearing my pajamas. I think they make a good undershirt." Tiffany, realizing she was in an assumption that one should not wear pajamas in public, quickly retreated: "I agree, maybe I should wear my pajamas to school too."

It was Kip's adventurous spirit that broke Tiffany out of her conventional thinking. How do we create those break outs for ourselves? About any issue, ask "What assumptions am I making that limit what I can see and think?" Then, answer the question.

"Break Out!" can be used when you know you are resigned, cannot solve a problem, or feel stuck or stale in any situation, project, or organization. It is a way of altering your focus so new perspectives about old issues can come to light. By realizing that assumptions are thoughts that can be changed, you develop greater freedom for your playful mind. When you need to refresh your thinking, close your eyes and become aware of assumptions that are limiting the range of your ideas. Take a leading assumption, reject it, then run the bases in your imagination. New ideas will miraculously appear because you have invited playful mind onto the field!

By challenging your assumptions, you develop the awareness that allows you to escape your confinement and to make new choices. For example, what assumptions do you hold that may be limiting your ability to cultivate a more creative life? Think up an answer, then find a way to break out of your thinking prison.

Chapter 13

Think Playfully
Together Without Greed

Competition appears quite often in our creative encounters. One reason is that people want to get credit for what they say and do to improve their social status and reputation. Another is that the ego will naturally try to enlarge its size so it can feel good. When it makes creativity points, it feels like a winner. This is similar to the way a conventional game of tennis is played. When the players walk on the court, their goal is to make points by keeping the opponent at a disadvantage and, if possible, to put "the ball away." Many of us play the creativity game this way. Who can make the most points with an idea? Who can gain advantage for a win?

"Brain storming" is a well-known method of creating novel ideas, but there is usually a fair amount of competition between people to come up with the best ideas. To encourage playful mind, the notion of "brain stimming" is used, which is short for "brain stimulation." In a brain-stimming session, the goal is to nourish the creative thinking of each other, not to make points with ideas.

Brain stimming is mental massage. Instead of waiting for others to stimulate our creativity, we take responsibility for awakening our own playful minds. Co-creating with two or more people, we massage each other's minds. Brain stimulation encourages play, so novel ideas come to life like unusual characters in a comedy.

PLAYFUL MIND:
"When you massage me, I gladly create for you."

When we relax and pursue creativity for the fun and fulfillment of it, greed for acclaim is significantly reduced. We probably still want acclaim, but are more willing to share it with others. This inner change prepares us to effectively co-create ideas and solutions to problems with others.

Co-Creating Without Greed

The goal of co-creating is to expand the range of playful mind so novel ideas appear in abundance. When co-creating occurs, it is difficult to say who was responsible for the results at the end because it feels like a mutual achievement.

Rules for co-creating ideas (The new game of tennis):

■ Keep the ball in play. Instead of dominating play and trying to make points, move the responsibility for contributing new ideas back and forth. If one person controls the process, the ball is being held too long. Keep it in play.

■ Everybody plays and no one wins. When it is a two-person game, it is easy for both to be involved. When several people play, make sure everyone participates. Co-creating is based on everyone feeling the obligation to play without concern for making points or winning. It is a joint endeavor to create new ideas and, when everyone contributes, it becomes a shared achievement. If you are working in a group, select a person to guide the process to insure full participation. Otherwise, the extroverts are likely to dominate the game while the introverts become observers.

■ Play off another person's idea. Be stimulated by the ideas of others. As you hear an idea, play off of it.

■ Suspend judgment about the quality of the ideas while play is in progress. To encourage the full range of the ideas, avoid making negative judgments about the ideas that appear. It is fine to say "Good idea" to someone's comment, but "That's not very realistic" will stop play. The goal is to generate as many novel ideas as possible in a short amount of time.

■ Record your ideas. Use a large sheet of paper for jotting down ideas. If you are working with a partner, you can alternate recording ideas. If you are working in a group, there is usually one person with the ability to quickly record ideas while also participating freely.

Process for Partners (30 minutes): Sit with a partner and decide who will start. To experience keeping the ball in play and playing off each other's ideas, do the following word association exercise together. One person starts by saying the first word that comes to mind. The other person spontaneously and quickly offers an associated word. For instance, the first person says "wedding." The second person responds with "perfect." The first person might then say "impossible." The partner then quickly plays off the word "impossible." Stay with the exercise until you feel the flow of the game and the playfulness of mutual brain stimulation. A few minutes is often enough time. Have fun!

PLAYFUL MIND:
"Having fun adds the bubbles to life."

Having experienced the flow of co-creating through the word association exercise, you are ready for a more challenging game called "Creat-a . . . ." "Creat-a" will help you develop new ideas about any topic. Working with your partner or group, select one of following topics or choose one of your own.

Creat-a wedding that is inexpensive and fun.
Creat-a new friend within a month.
Creat-a design for a workplace that would be inviting.
Creat-a vacation that is inexpensive and educational.
Creat-a way to retire that is unique.

Taking your topic, practice co-creating ideas.

■ Keep the ball in play.
■ Everybody plays and no one wins.
■ Play off another person's idea.
■ Suspend judgment about the quality of the ideas while play is in progress.
■ Record your ideas.

After recording your ideas, circle all your best ones, then design a plan of action.

If you are working in a group, partners share their results. When ideas are being presented, group members are free to play off those ideas.

Your capacity to co-create with others without greed will

make creativity a lot more fun and rewarding for you. Used on a regular basis, co-creating can transform the culture of an organization, how people relate to each other, and how problems are solved. As an alternative to competition and winning, co-creating together acknowledges and calls forth the abundant creativity in everyone.

SIGN ON THE WALL OF A SPORTS TEAM:
Two goals: Win, then keep winning.

SIGN ON THE WALL OF A CREATIVE PERSON:
Two goals: Create, then keep creating.

PLAY TIME!

Note three things you could create in your life this week that would make you happy.

Do them!
Do them!
Do them!

Chapter 14

PLAN IN A NOVEL WAY

When determination to achieve a goal is strong, the next step is to design an effective plan of action. As an example, we turn to the creativity of Walt Disney. He set in motion a form of innovation that produced films and theme parks that draw large crowds today. How did he achieve that success? He developed a simple strategy for creating novel ideas and producing successful results. At his film studios, he created three distinct rooms: A dream room, a planning room, and a critic's room.

At Disney Studios, the dream room nourished imagination and fantasy. Many innovative ideas emerged because the staff were encouraged to push the limits of their imagination and to dream up strange ideas. Nonsense and whimsy were fully honored. When a dream had been carefully developed, it was moved to the planning room where a plan was sketched out, then designed in great detail. When the plan was fully developed, it was moved to the critic's room. Taking on the role of critics, the staff carefully evaluated all aspects of the plan. They examined its logic, explored its inconsistencies, and identified areas that needed more careful design.

With definite ideas for revision, the staff might revisit the dream room to modify the fantasy theme or return to the planning room to revise and enhance the plan. Before a project was completed, they might circulate through the rooms several times. Based on their work in those rooms, the projects that emerged from Disney Studios were so imaginative and well-designed the chances of success were high.

While the following work in the three rooms of Disney is set up for an individual, it can easily be adapted for partners or a group. Visit the rooms together, co-create ideas, and develop an effective plan of action. You can also work as individuals and share your plans at the end.

Dream Room

Most of us fail to dream effectively. We get a vague idea of what to create, but stop short of filling in the specifics. In the dream room, the point is to dream carefully, so all the features of the dream are fully developed. You have dreamed carefully if you can see the details of the dream fully realized. When a dream is well developed, planning is much easier. Vague goals produce vague plans and work against success.

PLAYFUL MIND:
"Imagine that you had no imagination.
If you had no imagination,
how could you have imagined that?"

Individual Process (25 minutes): In your journal, put "Ideas from the dream room." Imagine yourself in a dream room that inspires fantasy and imagination. Touched by the spirit of the room, begin dreaming up new ideas for creative projects, note them, then return to the dreaming process.

When you have completed imagining projects, circle two or three that most inspire you. Put a star by your most compelling dream.

Explore all facets of that dream. How will it appear when it is realized? Whatever your dream, describe it fully.

Note the date when you want that dream to be a reality.

Planning Room

When entering the planning room, you call up your ability to create an effective strategy of action.

Making a plan is like taking a vacation.
First, you have to decide where you are going,
then you have to figure out how to get there.

Individual Process (40 minutes): Use a large piece of paper for designing your plan. Imagine being in a room that stimulates your planning instincts. What does it look like? Are there special features of the room that awaken your planning mind?

Remaining in the spirit of that room, start by establishing a time line. Recall the target date you set for realizing your dream. Record it at one end of your paper. From there, create segments of time. For example, if you are committed to having your goal achieved in one year, create 12 time segments, one for each month of the year. If you want to achieve it in one week, set up seven segments to correspond to the days of the week.

Plan in detail. Like our penchant for vague dreaming, many of us fail to take the time to plan carefully. Create a realistic plan that increases your probability of success. Martha had finished her plan well before any of the others, so I approached her with a question: "Do you have a plan that will really work?" "Sure do," she responded with confidence. As I began to examine her strategy, a glaring flaw jumped out. The first element of her plan was winning the state lottery.

When your plan is complete, return to the present. Note steps you will take today or tomorrow to achieve your goal. What specific steps will launch you into action?

Critic's Room

Entering the critic's room, establish access to your capacity for evaluation. What parts of your plan seem sound? What parts are questionable? Does the plan work as a whole? Imagine reviewing your plan with the same critical eye that you use when critiquing your appearance before an important public event.

Individual Process (20 minutes): Close your eyes and imagine a critic's room that will call forth your ability to carefully review, criticize, and suggest changes in your plan.

What deletions, additions, or modifications seem necessary? Note those.

If you are working alone but with a partner or group, share your plans. Ask for advice to improve them. Revise if necessary.

When you combine a well-designed plan of action with the ability to stay in momentum, you become a powerful force for innovation, effectiveness, and success.

> *Instead of fearing and avoiding criticism,*
> *embrace it like you would your best friend.*
> *Then, like a good friend, it will help you.*

Chapter 15

Becoming Unstoppable

*E*ven with a well-developed plan, obstacles are likely to get in our way. Some might be unexpected circumstances that work against us; others can emerge from our own thinking. We may become discouraged by thoughts such as "I have no talent for this" or "I don't see how this strategy will succeed." By learning to stop those kinds of thoughts from stopping us, we are able to maintain creative momentum, which dramatically increases the probability of our success over the long term.

Thoughts are like bubbles coming to the surface of boiling water; they are constantly emerging into awareness without our control. Thoughts affect our feelings and behavior. We cannot stop having thoughts, but their truth can be questioned. What if, instead of thinking our thoughts were true, we experienced them as just thoughts?

Individual Process (30 minutes): Close your eyes and observe your thoughts for five minutes. As each thought arises, think "Just a thought, not true, just a thought." Feel yourself coming into a new relationship with your thoughts. Take control of them so they give up their control over you.

PLAYFUL MIND:
"Put yourself in the saddle.
Learn to ride your thoughts,
not the other way around."

Identify something you would like to create. Tear up a piece of paper into six parts. On each piece, write down a thought that could stop your creative momentum. Turn them face down.

There are three decisions you can make to stop thoughts from stopping you.

■ Remove the thought from your mind. Anytime a thought tries to stop your creativity, discard it.

■ Reverse the thought into its opposite. You stop a thought from stopping you by reversing it so it becomes a positive thought to support your creativity. "I don't think I can do this" becomes "I think I can do this."

■ Replace the thought with any positive thought of your choice. "I'm so bored with my work" might become "Today, I'm going to look for a hidden opportunity."

Turn over your first slip, read the thought aloud, then make a decision to remove it, reverse it, or replace it. Speak your decisions aloud so you can hear yourself stopping the thoughts that would normally stop you. Repeat the process with your remaining thoughts, selecting different decisions to discover how each one works. If you are working with a partner or group, take turns reading a thought that stops you, then declare how you will put a stop to it. Use all three options. Share insights with each other at the end.

*"What if every time you heard a thought say 'Stop',
you automatically laughed, then said 'Go'?"*

Being Unstoppable Gives Us Time To Learn

One reason people fail to develop skills or reach their goals is that they listen to the thoughts that tell them they are unable do it. Thinking their negative thoughts are true, they quit trying, so they fail to give themselves enough time for learning, effort, and change. Anytime we make a commitment to develop new talents or achieve an objective, we recall the four principles of creativity:

Do,
Get feedback through "mistakes,"
Learn from the feedback,
Change what you are doing.

Making mistakes is an essential part of learning a new skill or realizing a dream. Instead of thinking they are proof that we have no talent or will fail, we regard the mistakes as helpful indicators of what we need to change or practice. Many people back out of creative activities and projects too early. They fail to give themselves enough time to make the mistakes that will eventually elevate their level of effectiveness.

PLAYFUL MIND:
"Mistakes are feedback
to brain, ear, and eye,
so they can do better
on the very next try."

Giving up too early is one reason we fail to realize our dreams; an unrealistic time scale is another. Some people believe that they should be able to draw, be effective speakers, good writers, or skillful teachers in an unrealistically short time. They forget that those whom they revere as artists, teachers, or performers worked hard over many years, making and correcting hundreds of mistakes, before attaining their high levels of skill. It was reported that Beethoven became furious after performing one of his piano concertos when an admiring fan called him a "true genius at the keyboard." He was reputed to have said quite gruffly: "You would be a keyboard genius too, if you spent 40 years practicing."

When you feel stuck,
name what is stopping you as a thought.
Once you know it is just a thought,
you can discard or alter it.

Learning to become unstoppable is important for cultivating a more creative life. It establishes the constant forward momentum that gives you time to pursue your dreams and, through effort, to realize them. Kristin had a life-altering discovery when she realized the power of thoughts to stop her. From her early teens she had been fascinated with the art of makeup and had secretly harbored a dream of becoming a makeup artist in Hollywood. She discovered three thoughts blocking her way. "People will think I'm not a liberated woman if I pursue a career in makeup." "This is a childhood fantasy I don't have the talent to achieve." "My parents will think I'm crazy."

When she realized that these were just thoughts stopping her, she threw them out and moved into action. She openly declared her intention to move to Hollywood to start her career and she received the support of her parents. Two years later she was a guest in my class, sharing impressive photographs of her work and describing how she had created a career as a freelance makeup artist in the film capital. She was successfully pursuing her dream and loved what she was doing.

Creative Project Check-In

Take a moment to evaluate your progress. If you have not started your creative project yet, what is one thing you could add to or subtract from your thinking to get going? How can you put a stop to any thoughts that are stopping you? If you are well underway, consider what your efforts are adding to your life. What are you noticing as your creativity expands and flourishes?

If you are working with a partner or group, share your progress with each other or get support if commitment is weak and progress is lagging.

You will need two balloons for the next chapter.

Chapter 16

BE RECEPTIVE TO COACHING

A supervisor asked Susan if she could take criticism. "No, I can't" she said without thinking. Her boss said nothing and walked away. She continued to think about that incident after several years because she was still curious about what he wanted to say. She knows that she missed the coaching. Sensitive to criticism, many of us put up resistance to coaching from others. We turn away, fail to really listen, become defensive, or counterattack, and therefore miss the feedback that could have made us more creative and effective. Fortunately, there is another way to respond to what we call "criticism."

> *TO EXPAND CREATIVITY, LIVE FOR THREE THINGS:*
> **Feedback, learning, and change.**
> **From those three comes a fourth:**
> **Effectiveness.**

Individual Process (10 minutes): In your journal, describe how you feel when someone criticizes you and your work. What is your automatic response? What do you say to yourself about the person criticizing you and the overall situation?

Note in a few sentences how your listening would change if you interpreted criticisms as "coaching."

Briefly describe how you would listen if, instead of thinking the criticism was pointing up a failure, you thought "This is just feedback for me to consider."

Write a few sentences explaining how your listening would change if you interpreted the person's communication as a "gift" rather than "gripe."

Describe how you might listen if you interpreted what was being said to you as an "opinion" to consider rather than the "truth."

If you are working with a partner or group, share what you discovered.

When criticized, many people interpret what is said as an "attack," "personal failure," or "gripe." This depends on the person offering the criticism and how they perceive that person's motives. If they interpret the motives as negative, they are more likely to respond aggressively or take a defensive position to fend off the attack. In an attack or defense posture, their ability to listen for information that person wants to convey stops. Without receptive listening, they miss the coaching, which undermines their potential to learn.

To become more coachable, change your interpretations from:

"criticism" to "coaching,"
"failure" to "feedback,"
"gripe" to "gift," and
"truth" to "opinion."

When we realize that creativity is about learning, change, effectiveness, and results, coaching becomes essential

because it is a type of teaching. We become learners looking for teachers to help us evolve. "Who can teach me new
skills and how I can be more effective at what I do?" are the
eager questions of a creative person. How the learning
takes place is through openness to feedback and careful listening.

PLAYFUL MIND:
"When receiving criticism,
imagine that you are a
gigantic ear without emotions."

A Shrinking Ego Stops Listening

Our aversion to criticism develops because it deflates our
egos, which makes us feel bad. When Susan told her boss
that she could not take criticism, she was really saying: "I
don't want to feel little and bad, so don't criticize me and
make me feel that way." What is fascinating about this
response is that it is automatic. Once the involuntary nature
of our response to criticism is understood, it is possible to
stop our egos from deflating, so we can listen carefully to
the feedback.

Individual Process (15 minutes): You will need two balloons for this process. Tear up a piece of paper into eight
parts.

On four slips, record compliments that someone might
make to you.

On the other four, note criticisms you might receive.

Turn the slips face down, mix them, then put them in a pile

in front of you.

Blow up a balloon until it represents the size of your ego when it is feeling good. Turn over your first slip and read it aloud. Blow air into your balloon if the statement makes your ego feel bigger. Let air out if the statement makes it feel smaller.

Move through your slips following this process, letting air in and out of the balloon as you feel your ego expanding and contracting in response to compliments and criticisms.

Just as in life, you may have a string of compliments or criticisms, so your balloon may become quite large or small. Have an extra balloon available in case the first one pops because of ego-inflation.

Variation for Partners or a Group (20 minutes): Sitting with a partner, exchange slips. Each partner should shuffle the slips and place them face down. With balloons inflated to the "feeling good" point, alternate back and forth. First one and then another will speak the statements as if someone were really saying them, while the partner blows air into the balloon or releases air in response to what is heard. At the end, share what you learned.

There is a way to prevent the deflation of our egos so we can listen more fully to coaching. Although most of us do not use it consciously, we use a "recovery claim," a positive statement we make in a moment of adversity to restore our self-confidence. Believing the statement to be true, it helps us recover our ego size. For example, "I know I'm a good person" is a reaffirming thought that some people use when faced with criticism or after failing to perform up to their standard.

Individual Process (15 minutes): On a journal page, spend a few minutes writing recovery claims that you could use when you are being coached. These are statements you would say to yourself that would help you manage the size of your ego, so you could really listen rather than becoming defensive or going on the attack. "I'm good enough" and "I can learn from this" are examples of claims people have created.

Circle the claim that has the greatest capacity to stop your ego from deflating during coaching. You can circle more than one for different occasions.

Retrieve your slips and pick out the critical ones. Put them in a pile, shuffle them, and place them face down. Blow up your balloon again to represent your normal ego size. Turn over the first criticism and read it aloud. If your ego would deflate upon hearing such a comment, start letting air out of your balloon, then state your recovery claim aloud and adjust the size of your balloon accordingly. Repeat this process for each slip. You can use different claims as you move along to discover their effectiveness.

Variation for Partners and a Group (20 minutes): Establish partners, then exchange negative slips. Having your balloons ready at an average size, alternate back and forth speaking your critical comments to each other. If a comment would cause your ego to deflate, let air out of your balloon, then state a recovery claim and adjust the size of the balloon accordingly. Experience your ability to manage the size of your ego, so you can be fully receptive to feedback. When you have completed the process, discuss what you learned.

When people put up resistance to coaching, they involuntarily reject feedback without weighing its merits. This is

especially the case where the criticism makes them feel little, because they will automatically discount the ideas in
order to manage the size of their egos. "No, that's not a better way" may be their response when someone suggests a
change in their thinking or work. They make up their minds
so quickly out of ego-defense that they fail to seriously consider what is being given to them as suggestions for change.

PLAYFUL MIND:
*"Imagine that every idea you hear from
your coach is clothing you're eager to try on
so you can decide if you want to buy it."*

Seek Additional Information

When people are receptive to coaching, they are more likely to seek clarification and more detailed information from
a coach. "Could you say something more about . . . ?"
becomes a vital question in the repertoire of those who are
receptive to feedback. With greater openness and eagerness
to learn, they are also more likely to receive detailed coaching from others.

If you have coached someone who responded defensively to
your feedback, you probably did not provide the depth or
detail in your critique that you would have with someone
who was a receptive listener. Coaches hold back details
when the person being coached assumes a defensive or
offensive stance. Therefore, only the vague outlines of the
key points are communicated. This weakens the coaching
because it lacks depth and clarity.

There is no need to make choices about the feedback during

coaching. Our job is simply to listen carefully and try to understand. We avoid the automatic reaction: "Yes, you are right. I will do that," unless the idea is definitely one we want to try. We have the option of telling our coach that we need some time to think more carefully about the feedback. Most coaches will be so delighted with our openness that they will respect our right to ponder and weigh what has been recommended. Once we reflect on the options, it is wise to let our coach know what we decided. If we make changes based on the feedback, it will create the conditions for future coaching from that person. Great mentoring emerges when we are fully coachable.

Seek Positive Feedback

There are few good coaches because most people who try to help us focus mainly on our shortcomings. If our coach is typical and emphasizes what we need to change, we can ask for positive feedback. "What do you notice that I'm doing well?" Seeking a positive evaluation increases our receptivity to coaching, while it identifies what we are doing well, so it is reinforced. Asking for positive feedback adds balance to any coaching session, which makes mentoring more effective.

Seek Coaching

When we are genuinely open to coaching, we can seek coaches rather than passively waiting for them to appear. Knowing that feedback will contribute to our learning and effectiveness, asking for coaching becomes a creative practice.

A coachable person will get more help than
someone who is resistant to coaching
and will learn more, change more,
and become more effective and successful.

Individual Process (15 minutes): Spend a few minutes thinking about people whose coaching you would value. Identify their names in your journal and briefly note what you would like to learn from them. Circle the name of at least one person and set a date when you will seek coaching.

If you are working with a partner or group, discuss how you will seek and be receptive to coaching.

The steps for becoming coachable are:

Step one: When someone says something that seems like "criticism," think of it as coaching, feedback, a gift, and an opinion. Avoid slipping into a defensive or attack posture, but remain open and accepting. Realize feedback is a point of view that might give you new information or a different perspective.

Step two: Establish ego size by using a recovery claim: "I can listen to and learn from this coaching because I know I'm a worthwhile person."

Step three: Once you establish ego size and receptivity, you will be in a better position to seek feedback in detail. Ask for clarification and more information. Do not judge what you are hearing, just fully hear it.

Step four: Know that no decision needs to be made while you are being coached. The point is to listen for choices and decide later. Be willing to try on all the ideas before making decisions about them.

Step five: Seek positive feedback that will help you understand what you are doing well. This will make the coaching more balanced and effective.

Step six: Thank your coach and let her or him know that you will think about the coaching and make some decisions.

Step seven: If you decide to change something based on the coaching, let your coach know. This will increase the likelihood of future coaching from that person.

Practice is crucial. Respond to coaching in the following week with the techniques you just learned. Actively seek coaching and remember to get positive feedback. How to become a more effective coach is next. If you are working alone, you will need a partner. Ask your partner to read and do the work in this chapter as preparation.

Chapter 17

BECOME A MORE EFFECTIVE COACH

*E*ffective teachers learn to engage and open the minds of their students. They are able to cultivate more attention and receptiveness to learning and change. Effective coaching is the ability to create that kind of attention and receptivity. It is productive teaching. How can we become more effective coaches, so others will want to hear and consider our ideas? To answer that question, you will need a partner.

Getting attention is much easier than cultivating receptivity to our ideas. Attention can be created by control, but receptivity never can. Receptivity arises when a coach is trusted to act in our interests. We impute good motives to a coach who demonstrates concern for our well-being. When that trust is present, listening and receptivity meet in a moment of heightened learning potential.

> *Good coaching arises from the desire to*
> *enhance the effectiveness of others*
> *in their work, their relationships,*
> *and their lives.*
> *It is based on caring.*

Individual Process (15 minutes): How would you like to

be treated by a coach? In your journal, note specific things the coach would do to make you receptive to feedback?

Examine what you have written as your blueprint for being a more effective coach.

Share your ideas with your partner. If you are part of a larger group, briefly communicate your discoveries.

Individual Process (50 minutes): Write a fairytale, starting with "Once upon a time." Establish freedom and fun as your inspiration points. Let the tale develop spontaneously. Take about 20 minutes for writing.

Exchange fairytales with your partner, so that coaching can begin. While reading your partner's fairytale, respond in writing to the following questions.

■ What do you like about the work? Be specific.
■ What would you change? Be specific.

What might be omitted?

What might be elaborated upon?

What might be changed in the story to make it more interesting or compelling?

What might be added?

■ What else do you like about the work? Be specific.

Notice that these questions are arranged like a sandwich: Affirmation on the top and bottom, suggestions as filling in the middle. This novel approach to evaluation is used in Toastmasters International, an organization that provides opportunities for becoming an effective public speaker. It is called the "Sandwich Technique."

Once you have finished writing your feedback, decide who will be coached first. Switch roles after the first round of coaching. Consider reviewing the steps in the last chapter for becoming coachable and apply them when you are being coached.

A principle to follow while you are coaching:
The person coached must be, at a minimum,
the same ego size he or she was
before you started coaching.
Bigger, if possible.

What do you need to know in order to be a more effective coach? Following are the key steps. Going through the steps may seem artificial, but it is good practice.

Step one: Ask the person if she or he would like your coaching and feedback. This will establish the kind of receptive listening you want.

Step two: Let the person know that you are offering coaching to improve results. Show that you care for the person's well-being and success.

Step three: Tell the person that you are offering only your viewpoint and it is up to him or her to evaluate it and determine what might be useful.

Step four: Use the "Sandwich Technique" for offering your feedback.

Using the Sandwich Technique helps a coach to recognize what a person is doing well and what can be improved. In this way, the feedback is balanced. Emphasizing what is being done well reinforces it. Adding suggestions opens up possibilities for change. Both increase effectiveness.

Examine what you wrote about your partner's fairytale. Notice that it is organized as a coaching sandwich. Use it to offer feedback in the following way:

First slice of bread: Provide positive feedback. What is the person doing well?

The meat or veggies: These are your various suggestions for change. Before offering them, let the person know that your feedback is a perspective that you hope is helpful. Then offer your suggestions as simply and clearly as possible.

Second slice of bread: End with more positive feedback. What else do you like about what the person has done?

Step five: Thank the person being coached for listening, then offer to be coached, so that coaching is established as something everyone needs.

Start the coaching process. For the person being coached: Practice being coachable as you listen to the feedback. If you feel your ego deflating, state a recovery claim to yourself so you can listen and be receptive. Ask for clarification if there is confusion. Seek more information, so you can practice wanting more depth and breadth of feedback. Coach, follow the steps for effective coaching. Feel yourself caring about your partner's well-being and effectiveness.

When you have completed being coached and coaching,

take time to reflect together. What did you learn? How will you use the methods? If you are working in a larger group, reconvene for sharing.

PLAYFUL MIND TO THE COACH:
"Instead of thinking you are the dart, imagine that you are the dart board that will receive your criticism."

A final point about effective coaching: On occasion, coach without the meat or veggies. When you notice someone doing something effectively, let that person know by first describing the good work you are observing. Add encouragement to your acknowledgment. When you recognize effectiveness and offer encouragement, you will help that person develop a foundation for future achievements.

Check Negative Emotions At The Door

While critiquing someone's performance or their work, we will feel a range of emotions. If our impressions are positive, we might feel happy, pleased, or satisfied. If our assessment is more critical, we may feel disappointed, irritated, or even angry. Sometimes, without being conscious of them, our negative feelings become a strong undercurrent in our feedback. If the person being coached senses our disappointment or anger, we are likely to receive a defensive reaction, hurt feelings, or a counterattack.

Unaware that our negative feelings were picked up by the person we were coaching, we may be caught off guard by the strong resistance we received to our suggestions. This unappreciative reaction may annoy us even further, which, if expressed, can produce a chain reaction of emotions between us. Before long, we may be shouting at each other. We may have started with the intention of being helpful, but undercurrents of our negative emotions polluted and ruined the session.

The point of coaching is to be helpful and clear. To achieve those goals, take a minute before you give feedback to honestly explore how you are feeling. If you become aware of negative emotions, "check them at the door" before the coaching begins. It will make you more effective.

*The person that you will coach
did not make the mistakes to annoy you.
They were made because of a lack of knowledge,
understanding, ability, or awareness.*

Being receptive to coaching and knowing how to coach effectively will increase your effectiveness and the performances of others. Being coached is an indispensable aid to the creative person who wants to become more successful. By being receptive to suggestions for change, you quickly gain new information and skills. By coaching others effectively, you help them listen attentively, develop new abilities, and achieve greater effectiveness and success.

*Effective coaches ultimately live for one thing.
That, one day, those they coach will surpass them.*

Chapter 18

ASK STRATEGIC QUESTIONS

*C*oaching emphasizes the importance of feedback, learning, and change. There is also a creative way of asking ourselves and others questions to encourage forward motion and change. In *By Life's Grace*, Fran Peavey calls this approach "strategic questioning." She reveals the crucial importance of asking strategic questions for motivating ourselves and others to change. Peavey's ideas about strategic questioning are briefly summarized with opportunities for practice.

■ A strategic question creates motion.

A strategic question helps people move into action. Perhaps there is a teenager who has a chronic problem of getting his homework done on time. A typical question might be "Why haven't you done your homework?" This question fails to create motion. It is a form of blaming that produces little or no change. A strategic question would be "What could you change so completing your homework is easier for you?" This question encourages motion and opens up the possibility of new solutions.

We can ask ourselves strategic questions to create motion. If we are contemplating a career change, we would avoid asking the question: "Can I successfully make this change?" Instead, we would ask a strategic question: "How can I successfully make this change?" The strategic question will make us aware of your resources and motivate us to plan our new career. There are people who make themselves miserable by continuously asking themselves "Am I interesting?" As a simple alternative, they could ask: "How am I interesting?"

Individual Process (5 minutes): In your journal, note a few strategic questions that would cause motion in your life or in someone else's.

■ A strategic question creates options.

A question can be useful if it reveals new possibilities. The teenager who fails to complete his homework could be asked: "What new approaches could you create to make doing homework easier?" For thinking about a new career change: "What are four novel approaches to starting a new career?" For the person who wants to become more interesting: "What are several different ways that I can become more interesting?" Strategic questions expand our awareness of options, so we automatically develop new ideas for action.

Individual Process (5 minutes): Record strategic questions that would create more options for you or someone else.

■ A strategic question digs deeper.

Strategic questions cause us and others to dig more deeply into issues. The teenager who fails to finish his homework could be asked to describe what goes through his mind as he is resisting. Anyone contemplating a new career could ask "What are my deepest fears as I consider this change?" The individual who wants to become more interesting might dig deeper into the issue by asking "What specifically makes someone interesting?"

Individual Process (5 minutes): Note a few strategic questions you could ask yourself or another person that would produce deeper digging.

■ A strategic question avoids "Why?"

"Why" questions can produce defensiveness and resistance. Yet, even when they produce such poor results, they are employed automatically and persistently. We might also blame ourselves by asking "why" questions. "Why am I so reluctant to start a new career?" "Why am I uninteresting?" "Why" questions force us to focus on the past rather the present and the future. They fail to mobilize our energies for action now.

In contrast to the deadening effect of "why" questions, our "how," "what," "where," and "when" questions cause motion and create options. For example, when there is a conflict in a relationship, a strategic question will encourage problem-solving: "How can we fix this problem together?"

Individual Process (5 minutes): Take a few "why" questions you ask yourself or others and convert them into "How," "What," "Where" or "When" questions.

■ A strategic question avoids "Yes" or "No" answers.

"Am I creative?" "Do I truly love others?" People ask these kinds of questions quite often. They are important questions, but they are risky. What if the answer is "No?"

Peavey recommends avoiding "Yes" and "No" questions. As an alternative, she suggests questions like: "How am I creative?" "When do I show love for others?" These questions avoid categorical replies and make us think more deeply about ourselves. In close relationships, a person would normally ask "Do you love me?" and then hope for a positive response. In contrast, strategic questioning creates more information: "What do you love about me?" "When do you feel the most love for me?"

Individual Process (5 minutes): Choose a few "Yes" and "No" questions you ask yourself or others and convert them into strategic questions.

■ A strategic question is empowering.

When questions generate awareness of options and reveal how change is possible, they empower us and other people to take action. Instead of asking "Can I make this change?" (a "Yes-No" question), we employ a strategic question, "What resources do I have to make the change I want?" Through strategic questioning, we empower ourselves and others to change. "What are four ways you could become happier? What are two steps you could take today?"

Individual Process (5 minutes): Develop a few strategic questions that would empower you or another person to take action.

■ A strategic question asks the unaskable.

There are questions that haunt us from the shadows. We are afraid to ask them because we are afraid of our answers. They are unaskable questions.

I have a bright, young friend who is dedicated to social change. At a family gathering, a relative asked her: "Has your effort to change the world made any difference?" This was a disturbing question because she had been afraid to ask it herself. After several days of painful reflection, her answer was "Yes." While giving a "Yes" or "No" answer to an unaskable question is an option, consider putting unaskable questions into their strategic form. "How has my effort to change the world made a difference?"

Individual Process (5 minutes): Identify an unaskable question and respond with an answer. Alter your question to make it strategic. How does it change your response?

If you are working with a partner or group, share your work for each part of strategic questioning. Discuss what you learned.

Strategic questioning adds the very important ingredient of creativity to social, organizational, and personal change. Knowing how to ask strategic questions becomes a key resource for the creative person. It can be applied to a variety of situations, including coaching sessions.

Changing Questions Changes Thinking

The human mind is obedient; it generally does what it is asked to do. The nature of a question makes a difference, because the mind will try to answer the question we ask. "Why am I so stubborn?" will lead to a list of reasons. "Am I capable?" will generate a "Yes," "No," or "Maybe" response. Strategic questioning gives the mind new instructions, so it must think with greater subtlety, flexibility, and creativity. "What are four ways that I could become less stubborn?" The mind will automatically provide options. "How am I capable?" will invite the mind to look for ways. By changing our questions, we alter the focus of our thinking and the resulting ideas.

PLAYFUL MIND:
*"When you ask creative questions,
I happily supply creative answers."*

Individual Process (15 minutes): Focus on an important issue in your life. In your journal, note some of the questions you have been asking yourself about it. Notice how those questions shape what your mind thinks about and says to you. What it says will affect your moods.

Next, design some strategic questions that will send your mind along new pathways.

Answer those questions briefly.

What new possibilities for change appear? Develop a new strategy for action.

If you are working with a partner or group, share your work.

You now understand the power of questions to shape the activity of your mind.

How will you use that understanding to improve your life and the lives of others?

---

*A child was heard saying to her mother:
"Mommy, how do you grow up and still have fun?"
Is your mind already seeking an answer?*

PLAY TIME!

Make up new questions to ask people
at parties and dinners
that will create interesting
conversations!

Deep Question:

Unusual:

Surprising:

Spiritual:

Now, let playful mind create a few.

Funny:

Poetic:

Weird:

Chapter 19

QUIT WHINING

Complaint arises from our resistance to the way that life occurs. We have an idea about how a situation should be and, when it fails to appear that way, we complain about it. Professional complainers are simply recording their frustration with the fact that life is unwilling to conform to their wishes. Without the wish that a situation should be a certain way, there would be no whining.

HOW TO STOP A COMPLAINT:
***Change the situation so it conforms to your
wishes. If it cannot be changed,
give up resistance to the way it is.***

Individual Process (40 minutes): Make four columns on a journal page. In the first, briefly note things you complain about.

In the second, note what your ego is trying to get from others with each complaint.

In the third, make a decision about whether the situation can be changed. Enter "Yes," "No," or "Maybe."

Looking at all your "No" responses, describe in column four what you will do to give up your resistance to what you cannot change.

When you give up your resistance, what happens to your complaint?

If you are working with a partner or group, share what you discovered.

In any aspect of life, awareness of a pattern can shift us out of automatic and into choice. Notice how conditioned our responses are when we are forced to do something we dislike or when a situation fails to conform to our wishes. Do we feel sorry for ourselves and begin complaining? Once complaining starts, it can ruin a whole day, a whole week, a whole life.

OBSERVATION ABOUT A CHRONIC COMPLAINER:
"If she gets into heaven,
she won't be happy there."

Turn Complaints Into Requests For Change

Some of us have reputations for being complainers and others whisper behind our backs about our constant whining. When we wake up to the fact that we are complainers, adding a small change in our behavior can make a huge difference. We can convert our complaints into requests for change. Instead of complaining about something and doing nothing, we go to the person who can alter the situation and request a change. Complaint is about the past; request is an opening to the future. Instead of starting with the statement "I have a complaint," we begin with "I have a request to make." Relationships of all kinds can be improved by converting our complaints into requests of change.

Individual Process (15 minutes): Return to column three of the work just completed. Focus on the complaints you make where change is possible. Take each one and shape it into a request for change.

Select one request that is especially important to you, then identify the person to whom you will make the request and the date by which it will be made. Follow through.

If you are working with a partner or group, share your new insights and decisions.

Complaint Partners

Living causes pressure to build within us each day. We have tasks to perform for which there is no enthusiasm. People make demands on us that are unrealistic. Often, the good work we do is not fully appreciated or even noticed. When pressures become unbearable, complaint is a way to relieve them. Let us be merciful and allow room for it. When we repress our complaints too much, they are likely to sneak up on us from behind with a vengeance.

While excessive complaining is unwise, there must be times and places to vent our pent-up feelings of frustration. One way to do this is to create a "complaint partner," someone who will listen to our complaints, give us sympathy, and confirm our view of the situation.

COMPLAINT SPEAKING:
*"It's about time you realized that
you can't get rid of me.
Get real! I'm one way you take
the pressure off and relax."*

Individual Process (15 minutes): In your journal, note the names of possible complaint partners. Select your best prospect. Determine a date by which you will try to set up a partnership.

Once you have a complaint partner, try using the technique "Let the kettle boil, but briefly." When either of you feels so frustrated you need to let off steam, spend no more than ten minutes complaining to your partner. After airing a complaint in that short time limit, expressions of sympathy and support should be offered. Take turns. Be sure you make each other feel justified in the complaint and comforted in the misery, which is what most of us want. When tension is released, consider taking a complaint and turning it into a request for change. Support each other in making those requests.

If you are working with a partner or group, reveal your possible complaint partners.

By developing a "complaint partner," complaints are confined to a limited time and place. This eliminates the gushing of complaints over a wide terrain which creates a reputation for being a "constant complainer" or "negative influence." While being passed over for a promotion and wondering why, others will know why but will not tell us. Complainers often remain in lower statuses because organizations cannot function well when those in responsibility are too negative in outlook. Also, complainers make themselves and others so miserable that life becomes a gloomy experience rather than a Technicolor adventure. If whiners fail to reform, they may discover that, when they get to heaven, they will not like it there either.

PLAYFUL MIND:
"Try whining with a smile on your face."

Chapter 20

How To Stop Procrastinating

*T*hings come into being through effort. The ability to work hard generally produces a payoff, whether writing a book, organizing a project, creating a company, designing a home, or improving a relationship. Staying in creative momentum marshals our many resources to get things done over time. Our effectiveness increases when we can accomplish good results with the least expenditure of energy. How that is accomplished is part of the creative equation of learning to think and behave in new ways. In contrast, procrastination can be the norm for some people. They resist what they must do and lose energy that could be used for creative purposes. Learning to put a stop to procrastination is part of becoming a more creative and effective person.

I Can Do It Later

Postponement of unpleasant tasks creeps into many parts of our lives. "I can do it later" is often the phrase we use to put off acting now. At work, the consequence may be an unfinished report that keeps making its way to the bottom of our "to do" pile. In households, "I can do it later" might mean that rooms do not get cleaned often enough or taking out the garbage becomes a struggle.

Recently, I had an interesting conversation with a graduate student who I had been told was a persistent procrastinator. Within the first few minutes, she provided four reasons why she was not ready to write a paper whose due date was imminent. "I'm confused about what to say," "I can't narrow down the topic so it's manageable," "I'm afraid to take a risk for fear of what the professor will say," "I'm not ready to write because I have to first review what I've read." As I listened, it became clear that, by thinking her procrastination thoughts were true, she had invented a compelling justification for not writing. It was obvious that she was strongly resisting having to do a job she found unpleasant, which was causing her a lot of stress and guilt. Imagine the amount of creative energy she was losing through her resistance.

Individual Process (20 minutes): In the middle of a journal page, write "Thoughts that come to me when I procrastinate." Recall a situation when you put off completing a task. Perhaps it is occurring now. Around the page, note thoughts that provided you with a good justification to do nothing. Add your thoughts of judgment for procrastinating, such as guilt, self-condemnation, self-pity, or even relief. Experience your thoughts as parts of a drama in your mind.

Standing in front of a mirror, act out your drama. It might begin, "Today is too beautiful a day to waste writing a letter. You can do it later." Does a judgment follow? As you make your way through your procrastination thoughts and judgments, reveal the drama that occurs when you procrastinate. Cut loose and have fun!

Repeat the drama until you have a deeper understanding of your procrastination pattern. At that point, write a short poem to capture what you learned. Looking into the mirror, read the poem to yourself. Keep repeating the poem until the ideas sink in. Note your discoveries.

Process for Partners or a Group (20-30 minutes): Start by working as individuals. Tear a piece of paper into six slips. Remember a time, past or present, when you put off doing a task. On separate slips, note the different thoughts you had. They can include thoughts that justified postponement or judgments that you made about yourself or the situation. Think of your writing as developing a movie script. What thoughts make up your internal procrastination drama?

If you are working with a partner, improvise a drama that reveals how a mind thinks when procrastination occurs. Decide whose mind will be explored first. That person will be "A", the partner "B." Exchange slips. Before starting, create a space where action as well as dialogue can occur. "A" begins the drama by expressing frustration with having to complete an unpleasant task. With the slips of "A" in hand, "B" begins speaking and acting out the thoughts of "A" as if they were lines in a drama. Getting into the spirit, "A" enters the dialogue, responding dramatically (perhaps with a hint of desperation or guilt) to what "B" has said. Working as a team, they perform the comedy, "Putting It Off, or A Saga of Pain and Loathing." After the final curtain, the process is repeated with "B" as the focus.

At the end, the partners share what they learned about procrastination from experiencing their minds as dramas.

If you are working with a group, follow the process above, but with slight variations. One volunteer starts by handing her or his slips to others in the group. That person opens the scene, then spontaneously interacts with group members who act out the thoughts on the slips they received. When the curtain falls on that drama, others follow until everyone's procrastination drama has been performed.

Afterwards, discuss what you learned about "I can do it later."

Understanding procrastination as a mental drama can create a shift in your thinking toward more effective action. What will help you to create a permanent change is the development of a practice that overcomes your lethargy by insisting on immediate action.

Listen to the General!

When people have little desire to do something, resistance, complaint, and procrastination set in like mental arthritis. Learning to respond to the General overcomes this resistance and things get done. In the movie "Twelve O'clock High," Gregory Peck plays a general who is assigned the task of renewing the commitment of a group of pilots during World War II. Each time he gives a command, his subordinates are required to respond with "Yes, Sir!" and then they get the job done.

To launch into action when desire is absent, try practicing "Listen to the General!" When you find yourself resisting or complaining about a job you must do, say to yourself, "Listen to the General." He or she will say: "I order you to . . . ." Then, respond by getting the job done. You can also invent a practice that is uniquely your own.

Individual Process (10 minutes): Invent a creative strategy that will move you into action when you are resisting doing a job. Then, invent a command, such as "Listen to the General," that will help you overcome your resistance.

If you are working with a partner or group, share your

strategies and commands.

Laurie, a long-time procrastinator, put a stop to it by design-ing a simple practice from this work. Every time she catch-es herself putting off what she must eventually do, she says: "One, two, three, Go!" "I can't believe what I accomplish now," she said. "It's so much easier to just do it instead of wasting energy resisting doing it. One, two, three, Go! launches me into action."

> *Effectiveness increases when we quit resisting*
> *what we have to do. We put energy that*
> *would have been lost through resistance*
> *into constructive effort, so things*
> *get done more easily.*

Commands, such as "Listen to the General" or "One, Two, Three, Go!", will help you stay in momentum to finish tasks when your desire is weak or absent. It can also help you complete projects where you have lost enthusiasm. You waste time and energy resisting what eventually has to be done. So, why not move into action? Notice how deli-catessen employees respond to their customers. They call the next number and fill that order without resistance. As a consequence, they accomplish a lot in a short period of time. Consider using this "delicatessen approach" to get things done when you have no desire to do them. "Next!" is another motivational practice to try out.

A retired corporate executive who was instrumental in building a highly successful company was asked: "What are the most important ingredients of success?" "Two things," he said. "The first is hard work. The second is hard work." This emphasis on effort is nicely expressed in the popular idea,

"Creativity is ten percent inspiration and ninety percent per-spiration."

PLAYFUL MIND:
*"Don't expect to get anywhere
if you're unwilling to pedal the bike."*

PLAY TIME!

Take
a
walk
around
your
neighborhood,
noticing
things
you have
never
noticed
before.

Find the
hidden
wonder.

Chapter 21

Random Connections Surprise The Mind

"How is your life like a block of wood?" "What? There's no way I can see the connection between a piece of wood and my life." This was Lynn responding to my question. "Okay," I said, "pretend you are holding a small block of wood in your hand. Let the playful part of your mind generate ideas about your life by experiencing that small piece of wood."

Somewhat reluctantly, she began: "Well, my life is like this small block in the sense that it has dimensions. In fact, there are more sides to it than meet the eye. Sometimes I'm really dense, like the wood, and I don't recognize how, by my choices, I'm messing up my life. I'm quite useful and when someone drives a nail in me it hurts and the hole stays forever. I have quite a few holes and I think about them a lot. Maybe I think about them too much, instead of living my life in a better way."

I watched as Lynn's eyes revealed a deepening awareness about her life. Then, she looked at me in surprise and said, "I can't believe that I just learned something about my life from a block of wood!"

Individual Process (10 minutes): Put an imaginary block of wood in your hands. Using playful mind, let it teach you something about your life. Establish the intention of producing a novel change in your understanding. Record your insights.

If you are working with a partner or group, share your discoveries.

By exploring commonalities between things that make little sense to the mind, you will surprise it, which will encourage it to play. "How is your career a tree?" "How is your capacity for happiness like a snowball?" Any ideas?

PLAYFUL MIND:
"You've heard that "Life is like a bowl of cherries," but what if it was like a banana?"

Object Play

Most people are unaware of the large number of objects that lie close at hand as potential sources of inspiration. Imagine that you are sitting at a desk. It might hold a computer, printer, a cup, a telephone, a pen, a nail, a stack of paper, or a telephone book. As objects, each can introduce playful possibilities for your mind. In Object Play, things that you can touch, smell, see, taste, and hear are used to stimulate your thinking so new ideas appear.

How Object Play works: Imagine that your topic is how to improve the way a friend listens to you. Pick up a nearby object on the desk; for example, the nail. Let your thinking be stimulated by that simple object. "The nail reflects light. Maybe I need to think in a more enlightened way about this issue? Am I listening carefully? Am I clear enough in my communications? What if my friend and I spent some time together sharing how we talk and listen with the idea of enlightening each other?"

Having developed some ideas from the reflected light on the nail, a new object would be taken from the desk to cultivate other ideas about the listening issue. What thoughts would emerge by using the computer as a source of inspiration? Object to object, you discover new ideas, then select your most promising ones. From those, you develop a strategy for action.

Individual Process (30 minutes): Collect several objects together and choose a topic. Maybe you are a teacher and have a lesson plan to create. Perhaps you need to develop a new fund-raising strategy for your organization. Record the issue in the middle of a page and take an object from your collection. Let your playful mind be inspired by the object, generating ideas and noting them.

When that object has exhausted its many possibilities, select another to stimulate your thinking. Repeat the idea-generating process.

Select a third object to discover what novel ideas it will produce for you. Work for surprises and shifts in thinking.

Circle your most promising ideas and examine a few discarded ideas for hidden gems. Convert one into a viable idea.

If you are working with a partner or group, share your results.

PLAYFUL MIND:
"Objects are my toys.
When you change what you
give me to play with,
I change what I give you back."

Optional Group Process (50 minutes): If you are in a large group, divide into small groups of three or four people. Have participants sit in a circle, around a small table if possible. Discuss possible topics where you would welcome new ideas. Select one for the process.

Seek a volunteer in the group to record ideas on a large piece of paper. Have someone pick up a nearby object. Objects in pockets or purses are always good prospects. Pass the object around the circle, each person using it to develop novel ideas about the topic. Suspend judgment and have fun.

When you are ready to shift your thinking, select another object and repeat the process.

Select a third object to discover what new ideas it stimulates.

At the end, circle your best ideas and design an approach to your issue. If you are working in a large group, small groups should share their results.

A Paper Bag Is Useful

To surprise the mind, use a paper bag as a creativity tool. It becomes the container for placing ideas, bits of information, pictures, or whatever else you want to add for making chance connections.

■ When you need to create ideas for redesigning an organization:

Note various divisions or departments of the organization on slips of paper. Add key roles. Place them in the bag and shake the contents. Without looking, select two items to produce a chance connection. Perhaps you have chosen the accounting department and the role of custodian. Let playful mind create ideas from that surprising combination.

Select another item from the bag to add to the existing pair. How does your thinking change when a new item appears? What novel ideas arise?

■ When you need ideas for writing:

On slips of paper, record ideas about life and images that have emotionally moved you. You can add pictures cut from magazines. Put them in your bag. Draw out two items. If you have randomly selected a picture of a child laughing and the idea "job," what will you write from this chance connection?

You can use this technique for generating ideas for other works of art, like drawings, paintings, sculptures, dances, musical compositions, and architectural designs.

■ When you need ideas for a new product within your company:

Identify the names of products your company has already developed. Add the names of related products that are out on the market. Put them in a bag, shake them, and select two items. Imagine your company produces garden supplies and the products you selected are "hoses" and "shovels." What new ideas for inventions would this random connection produce?

These examples illustrate how to use random associations to cultivate novel ideas. Adapt the technique to your own needs. It is automatic to become fixed in our thinking and not notice it; using random connections is one way to loosen the mind and change your thinking.

One day, Sophia handed me a small gift before class. When I opened it, I was delighted to discover an elaborately decorated box that she had made. On top were written the words "Angel Cards." Inside, on small slips of paper, were words that she had written that, in combination, would alter someone's thinking and mood. Two cards I selected from the box were "openness" and "surrender." If those were your random choices, what new ideas would come to mind?

Each day, I took the Angel Cards to class, putting them on a small table where students gathered. When a student needed a change, Sophia's cards were used. They became a source of surprise and inspiration during the semester.

Impressed with Sophia's idea, Mindy made a box of "Love Cards" for her mate as a Valentine's Day gift. Each card was heart-shaped, with an expression of affection written in the center. One said: "You are the only person I would do laundry for." During times she was mad at him, he would take and read a "Love Card" to remind him that Mindy's anger was temporary but her love was deep and enduring. His regular use of the cards affected his thinking during those tense times, which prevented arguments.

Random choices surprise the mind. When caught off guard, it will play. When it plays, it adds flexibility to your thinking, so new ideas and approaches appear with little effort.

What thoughts would come to mind if you drew two Angel Cards? One said "release" and the other "joy?"

How would you feel if "You are wonderfully wonderful!" was your choice from Mindy's Love Cards?

One day, as I walked home after teaching, I saw a stone lying on the sidewalk. As I passed by, I noticed some writing on it, so I picked it up. My mood brightened immediately. Someone had written a message on the stone and put it on the sidewalk as a pleasant surprise for a stranger. It said "Don't worry, you are loved." Experiencing the positive effects of this act of kindness, I thought, "There are some wonderful people in the world." I put the stone down again, wanting someone else to feel as uplifted as I had been.

Chapter 22

A More Balanced Life Is Possible

Seeking acceptance, reputation, or simply wanting to keep their jobs, many people today stay late and work on weekends. They may not like it, they probably complain about it, but they do it anyway. They conform to unreasonably high standards of commitment rather than stand firm and draw a line: "No more than this" or "No, I won't do that." By drawing a line, creating a more balanced life becomes possible.

Our lives are shaped by choices, including our simple "Yes" and "No" responses to requests for our time and energy. If we say "Yes" too often, our commitments can grow to be so heavy that life becomes a strenuous endurance test rather than an opportunity for well-being and enjoyment.

PLAYFUL MIND:
"If you decide to get behind the wheel,
you get to drive the car."

How Balanced Is Your Life?

We are governed by opposing tendencies that pull us one

way and then the other. We need to be active but also long for rest. We need challenge but also relief from it. We are of two minds about many things and we struggle with the natural tension of the opposites within our thinking. When heavy commitments throw our lives out of balance, one side of us dominates the other. Wisdom is the capacity to honor both sides so balance improves. With better balance, stress is significantly reduced, so life becomes easier and more enjoyable.

Individual Process (35 minutes): Are you satisfied with the balance of commitments in your life? To answer this question, place an "X" on each scale that roughly represents the percentage of time you spend in that activity during a typical week.

| 0 | 10 | 20 | 30 | 40 | 50 | 60 | 70 | 80 | 90 | 100 |

Career work/job

School work

House/yard work

Cooking

Child care

Personal growth

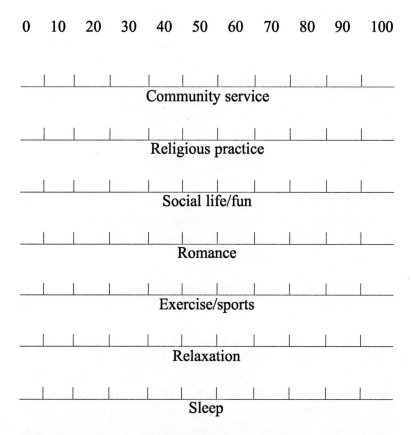

0   10   20   30   40   50   60   70   80   90   100

Community service

Religious practice

Social life/fun

Romance

Exercise/sports

Relaxation

Sleep

Take a moment to reflect on your use of time. What areas of your life seem out of balance?

Using that awareness, make new choices. For each activity, put a circle on the continuum that reflects the amount of time you would like to spend.

Write a note in your journal describing what you will add to and subtract from your life to create more balance. What specific steps will you take to make the change? Note those. What first step will you take today?

Recess of the mind: Take a few minutes to reflect on your discoveries. Imagine living the more balanced life that you want. What did you do to create that kind of life?

If you are working with a partner or group, share what you learned and what you intend to change.

Say "No" Without A Crack In It

Telling the truth helps us create balance. Often the truth is known: Adding another commitment is unwise. By realizing that "No" is as good a choice as "Yes," "No" becomes a tool for creating a more balanced life.

Individual Process (10 minutes): For a few minutes, write about the question: "Why is it easier to say 'Yes' than to say 'No'?"

Briefly describe what risks you think you are taking by saying "No," then develop a simple strategy for saying "No" that would empower you to turn down a request and feel good about it. What personal resources could you use to draw a line and stand firm?

If you are working with a partner or group, share what you learned by addressing these questions, including your strategy for saying "No."

There Is A "Yes," "No," And "Gray Area"

There are times when "Yes" or "No" are spoken with conviction. Those are "feel good" decisions because our preference is clear. However, many requests fall into the "gray area," where it is unclear if a new responsibility will be a good growth experience or an important service. One reason "Yes" becomes our choice is this gray area of uncertainty. Being unsure, we say "Yes" to feel good or because giving a positive response will earn us respect or a reward. Sometimes there is no choice but to say "Yes."

When receiving a request for help, you may inadvertently leave an opening for the person trying to persuade you to take on a new responsibility. This opening is a "crack." The crack appears when you add a qualification to your response, such as "Maybe" or "I'd really like to help, but...."

People who make requests for your time and energy are not impartial. They want to mobilize you. They will listen for ambivalence. When they hear a crack, they will increase their efforts to convince you. Opening lines of their request may hook you at an emotional level. You may hear: "You are the only person qualified to do this job" or "You can really make a difference by taking on this responsibility." I am especially vulnerable to the opening line: "I have a very special favor to ask of you." This line often traps me into wanting to help because of the value I place on personal loyalty.

Individual Process (10 minutes): What opening lines have the tendency to set you up for a positive response when, truthfully, you would say "No?" Enter them in your journal.

If you are working with a partner or group, share the opening lines that hook you.

What options exist for responding to requests for your time and energy?

■ Say "No" and really mean it. (No crack)

■ Say "No, maybe," but really mean "No." (Crack)

■ Say "Yes" when you really want to say "No." (Big problem)

■ Say "Maybe" because of genuine uncertainty. You may feel there are reasons to say "Yes," but there is also a part of you that wants to say "No." (Genuine crack.)

■ Say "Yes" because you want to do it. (No Problem)

"No" Without A Crack Is Self-Protecting

Since saying "Yes" makes us feel good and saying "No" makes us feel bad, learning to say "No" without a crack is important. By learning that "Yes" and "No" are both valid choices, our flexibility to respond to requests increases. Knowing we are often of two minds, "Yes" and "No" become equally plausible responses to any request.

Individual Process (20 minutes): Think of a request you might receive in the future where the pressure will be to say "Yes," but you will want to say "No." If nothing comes to mind, recall a situation where you said "Yes" but wished you had said "No."

In front of a mirror, play the role of the person making the request. Would the opening line be a clever hook? Would compliments be a part of it? Make the persuasive argument that person will make.

When you finish hearing the request, respond by saying

"No" without a crack in it. If you want, add a brief comment to explain why you are declining the request, such as "Taking on a new responsibility would add too much stress to my job and make me ineffective." Your reason could contain exaggeration to add a note of humor. "Would you like an insane woman running through the halls?"

People typically want to give a reason for saying "No," but it is possible to just say "No." If you feel compelled to give a reason, make it brief. Longer explanations often end up revealing cracks because of guilt or ambivalence.

Continue the mirror process, experimenting with different ways to say "No." You can repeat the process with other requests for your time. Become more comfortable with your power to say "No." Remember, it is a choice that serves you.

Optional Group Process (30 minutes): If you are working with a partner or a group, try the following. Sit with a partner. Tell each other about a request that you expect to receive in the future to which you will want to say "No." If nothing comes to mind, share a time when you said "Yes" but wished you had said "No." Give enough detail about the situation and the person making the request so your partner can play the role of that person. Choose an "A" and "B."

"A" takes the role of the person making the request and offers an opening line to hook "B." "A" makes the request, giving reasons why "B" should respond positively. When the request has been made, "B" responds by saying "No" without a crack. "B" may give a brief reason for declining, but it should be brief, true, or funny. The job of "A" is to persuade "B" to take on the task. "B" continues to respond with a "No." If "B" reveals a crack, "A" continues trying to persuade. When "A" is confident that "B" really means "No," the exercise is brought to a close.

Switch roles. "B" becomes the person making the request. "A" practices saying "No" without a crack in it.

In closing, the partners share their experiences.

If this work is occurring in a larger group, everyone reconvenes for sharing.

Saying "No" is often difficult. It takes courage because saying "No" can make us feel guilty and afraid of punishment and rejection. Knowing how hard it can be, it is wise to build a network of support to create a more balanced life. Among a group of kindred spirits, a small and persistent voice emerges in the din of a society moving at top speed. You can hear the voice quietly repeating: "Not so fast, not so much."

Create a "Commitment Partner"

As a step toward having greater control over our commitments and lives, we can ask another person to be our "commitment partner." The responsibility of the partners is to make sure neither assumes so many commitments that life loses its balance.

Individual process (5 minutes): In your journal, note the names of people who might be good commitment partners. Circle your best prospect and note a date when you will ask that person.

If you are working with a partner or group, share who you will contact and when.

When the partnership is established, you will be required to consult your commitment partner before making a decision about requests for your time and energy. This arrangement introduces a creative way for you to respond to requests: "Before I can decide to take on this new responsibility, I'm obligated to consult my commitment partner." Like a good curve pitch in baseball, this may catch the other person off guard, "Okay, get back to me as soon as possible." As you consult with your commitment partner, you might discover enthusiasm for the assignment or that you are willing to do it as a service. You will also have time to prepare yourself to say "No" without a crack in it, if that is our preference.

Imagine yourself enjoying saying "No."

What did you add to or subtract from yourself to produce that unusual ability?

PLAY TIME!

Put on some music!

Close your eyes,
relax,
and let your mind and body dance
without moving your feet.

Chapter 23

LIVING A CREATIVE LIFE

*I*magine creativity permeating all aspects of your life. You know that you are a creative person. In any situation, you ask "What is the creative thing to do here?" Then you do it. You are able to remove or change any thought that stops your creative momentum. You enjoy the creative process rather than worrying so much about proving your personal worth through the results you achieve. You cultivate creativity wherever you see an opportunity, so that your life becomes more interesting, challenging, and fun. By cultivating a more playful mind, you have a more playful life.

What's In The Box?

Individual Process (1 minute): Close your eyes and imagine that you are looking at a small covered box on a table in front of you. "What's in the box?" Come up with as many ideas as you can in approximately one minute.

If you are working with a partner or group, share what you saw inside the box.

When people are asked "What's in the box?" wild suggestions arise spontaneously. "There's a stampeding elephant in there." "The whole cosmos is in there." "I'm in there."

"I can distinctly hear a marching band." These reactions are signs of playful minds in motion.

With a more playful mind, what do you want to create in your life now?

"Show and Tell"

If you are working with a partner or group, finish with "show and tell." Create a time to share what you did, without needing to prove anything. Invite some friends.

THE ABUNDANT GARDEN

The garden showed serious signs of neglect.
Without care and daily watering,
the plants had lost their creative spirit.
They no longer bloomed.

Knowing the garden could be restored
to its natural beauty and wonder,
the gardener began tilling the soil,
watering, weeding, and watching.

Soon the plants revived.
New branches formed, leaves quickly multiplied,
and buds appeared everywhere,
clear signs of new vitality and abundance.

Now the garden is in full bloom.
The gardener helped, but it was
the plants that brought the blossoms
into fullness of being again.

BIBLIOGRAPHY

Cameron, Julia. *The Artist's Way: A Spiritual Path to Higher Creativity.* New York: G.P. Putnam's Sons, 1992.

De Bono, Edward. *Lateral Thinking: Creativity Step by Step.* New York: Harper and Row, 1970.

Edwards, Betty. *Drawing on the Artist Within.* New York: Simon and Schuster, 1986.

Gardner, Howard. *Creating Minds: An Anatomy of Creativity Seen Through the Lives of Freud, Einstein, Picasso, Stravinsky, Eliot, Graham, and Gandhi.* New York: Basic Books, 1993.

Goldberg, Natalie. *Wild Mind: Living the Writer's Life.* New York: Bantam Books, 1990.

Hirshberg, Jerry. *The Creative Priority: Driving Innovative Business in the Real World.* New York: HarperCollins Publishers, 1998.

Lloyd, Carol. *Creating A Life Worth Living: A Practical Course in Career Design for Artists, Innovators, and Others Aspiring to a Creative Life.* New York: HarperCollins Publishers, 1997.

Peavey, Fran. *By Life's Grace: Musings on the Essence of Social Change.* Philadelphia: New Society Publishers, 1994.

Rico, Gabriele Lusser. *Writing the Natural Way: Using Right-Brain Techniques to Release Your Expressive Powers.* Los Angeles: J. P. Tarcher, Inc., 1983.

Sark. *Inspiration Sandwich: Stories to Inspire Our Creative Freedom.*
Berkeley: Celestial Arts, 1992.

Sark. *Living Juicy: Daily Morsels for your Creative Soul.* Berkeley:
Celestial Arts, 1994.

Sark. *Succulent Wild Woman: Dancing with your Wonder-full Self.*
New York: Simon and Schuster, 1997.

Von Oech, Roger. *A Whack on the Side of the Head: How to Unlock
your Mind for Innovation.* New York: Warner Books, 1983.

Von Oech, Roger. *Creative Whack Pack.* Stamford, CT: U.S. Games
Systems Inc., 1992.

Girls, Inc.

Girls Incorporated is a national nonprofit organization that inspires all girls to be strong, smart, and bold[SM]. With local roots dating to 1864 and national status since 1945, Girls, Inc. has responded to the changing needs of girls and their communities through programs and advocacy that empower girls to reach their full potential and understand, value, and assert their rights. Girls, Inc. public education extends the values of girls' rights to adults as well, giving them the tools they need to assist girls' efforts to access their rights.

Programs focus on science, math, and technology, health and sexuality, economic and financial literacy, sports skills, leadership and advocacy, and media literacy for girls ages 6 to 18 throughout the United States. While Girls, Inc. attempts to reach all girls, it recognizes that girls in at-risk communities have an even greater need for its programs. Of those it serves, a majority are girls of color, girls who come from single-parent households and from households with incomes under $20,000.

To learn more about Girls, Inc., access resources for girls, advocate for girls' rights, make a donation, or introduce a girl to activities that will inspire her to be strong, smart, and bold, visit its website [www.girlsinc.org].

About the Author

Jim Downton has taught at the college level for thirty-six years. At this time, he is a Professor of Sociology at the University of Colorado, Boulder. Teaching is one of his deepest commitments. He teaches undergraduate courses in human development and creativity and frequently offers workshops on creative teaching for graduate students and faculty. His commitment to innovative teaching has earned him the University's two teaching excellence awards. He is also involved in the International and National Voluntary Service Training Program (INVST) at the University of Colorado, an innovative leadership training program for upper division students that emphasizes civic responsibility and community service. To learn more about INVST, visit its website:[www.colorado.edu/ArtsSciences/INVST].

In the community, Jim offers workshops in human development and creativity. In addition to teaching and writing, he enjoys painting and sculpture. His life revolves around the issues of wholeness and creativity, which are ways of cultivating inner peace, happiness, and an easier way of living.

Printed in the United States
1540600006B/385